THE
FENDER
BOOK
TONY BACON & PAUL DAY

The Fender Book
A complete history of Fender electric guitars
By Tony Bacon & Paul Day

A BALAFON BOOK

First British edition 1992

Published in the UK by Balafon Books, an imprint of Outline Press Ltd, 115J Cleveland Street, London W1P 5PN, England.

ISBN 1-87-154754-7

A catalogue record for this book is available from the British Library

Printed in Hong Kong

Editor: Roger Cooper
Art Director: Nigel Osborne
Design: Sally Stockwell
Typesetting by Midford Limited, London W1
Print and Origination by Regent Publishing Services

CONTENTS

INTRODUCTION	4
THE FENDER STORY	8
REFERENCE SECTION	66
CHRONOLOGY OF MODELS	68
GUITAR DIRECTORY	70
DATING METHODS	91
INDEX	94
ACKNOWLEDGEMENTS	96

INTRODUCTION

Fender is probably the most successful and almost certainly the best-known manufacturer of electric guitars in the world. The development of the company's innovative products and its changing personnel make for fascinating reading, but until now there has been no chronicle of Fender's history from its origins to the present day.

This book covers the electric guitars produced by Fender, from the 1950s to the 1990s – Fender's bass guitars and amplifiers deserve the space and privilege of separate publications. We feel that all periods of Fender history are worthy of equal attention, and in this book you will find facts from the earliest to the most recent times.

The opening part of the book covers the history of the Fender company from the first years of struggle and innovation to Fender's present status as a major institution in the music industry. We have tried to be sceptical and yet open-minded in reconstructing accurate and realistic accounts of the key events in Fender's history, often using personal views from fresh interviews conducted with leading Fender employees, both past and present. Also here are superb colour photographs of fine guitars and memorabilia.

The second part of the book is a comprehensive reference listing of all Fender's production electric guitars from the USA, Japan and elsewhere, with concise information to assist in identifying and dating Fender instruments.

THE FENDER BOOK is designed as an honest appraisal of a unique, enduring American company. We enjoyed writing it and learned a lot in the process, and hope you'll feel the same once you've read it.

TONY BACON & PAUL DAY, ENGLAND, JUNE 1992

"Leo Fender was striving to do the very best that he could for musicianship, to make his products ahead of the pack, and he knew that the working musician was the secret to all of that."

Bill Carson, *WESTERN-SWING MUSICIAN, EMPLOYED BY FENDER SINCE 1957 (CURRENTLY DISTRICT SALES MANAGER FOR FIVE SOUTHERN STATES)*

"The Fender factory was Leo's temple, it was his place of worship."

Dale Hyatt, *FENDER SALESMAN, EMPLOYED BY FENDER 1946-1972*

"Even though Leo was not an engineer he was sharp mechanically, sharp as a tack."

Forrest White, *PRODUCTION CHIEF AT FENDER 1954-1967*

"Whether you agreed with Leo all the time or not, he usually wound up right."

Karl Olmsted *OF RACE & OLMSTED, FENDER'S TOOL-AND-DIE MAKER 1947-1983*

"I doubt you could go to any country on earth and they haven't heard of Leo Fender, and there's probably very few other men that fits that spot."

George Fullerton, *FENDER EMPLOYEE 1948-1970*

"Leo had this curiosity and nothing ever really satisfied it. There was always something more, something more. He just never was satisfied, he was always going to do something that little bit better."

Phyllis Fender, *LEO'S SECOND WIFE, MARRIED IN SEPTEMBER 1980*

"Leo was the Henry Ford of guitars."

Dan Smith, *JOINED FENDER AS DIRECTOR OF MARKETING, ELECTRIC GUITARS, IN 1981; CURRENTLY VICE PRESIDENT, MARKETING, ELECTRIC GUITARS*

Pictured above: A Fender advertisement from 1958 (top left), part of the company's much praised campaign based on the slogan 'You won't part with yours either'. A work area in the Fender factory is shown (top right), probably in 1966, with a Jaguar receiving final adjustment. Bob Perine, a Californian artist, was responsible for much of the illustration work in Fender's promotional material of the 1960s, and this example (above) is from the cover of the 1964/65 catalogue.

Pictured on opposite page, clockwise from top left: Don Randall, head of Fender Sales, pictured just after the sale to CBS in the mid 1960s; Forrest White, Leo Fender and George Fullerton are shown holding gifts at a Fender Christmas party in 1956; yet another yuletide gathering at Fender, this time in 1953 – the man looking up, smiling, is Freddie Tavares, behind his left shoulder is employee Louis Lugar, and behind him, in glasses, is Tadeo Gomez whose initials are sometimes seen on early Fender guitar necks; the ad showing Leo Fender ('this man started a revolution') was placed in the music press in 1972, two years after Leo had left the Fender company; and the gathering at the workshop table shows Doc Kauffman (left) and Leo Fender (right), behind whom is Leo's friend Ronnie Beers.

This Man Started a Revolution.

NO OTHER ORGANISATION has contributed more to the look and sound of the modern solid-bodied electric guitar than Fender. The company's simple, elegant designs grace millions of instruments – not only the huge quantities made by Fender themselves but also the countless copies made by other manufacturers throughout the world. Virtually every innovative pop musician has used a Fender guitar at some point, and the famous Fender logo has been a familiar sight to musicians from the country-and-western stage of the 1950s to the rock recording studio of the 1990s.

Clarence Leo Fender's original company changed the course of popular music by revolutionising the design and manufacture of electric guitars. So successful did the company become that in 1965 the Fender operation was sold to the giant CBS conglomerate for no less than 13 million dollars. Yet the whole affair had started some 20 years earlier when Leo made some electric steel guitars with a few thousand dollars earned from a record-player design. From these humble beginnings grew one of the largest, most influential and splendidly original musical instrument manufacturing companies in the world.

Despite spectacular later successes, during its early years the southern Californian company came perilously close to failing. It was Leo Fender's sheer determination combined with his luck in surrounding himself with clever, dedicated people which helped pull the Fender company through those difficult times.

Leo was born in 1909, in a barn near the Anaheim/Fullerton border in the Los Angeles area. His parents ran a truck farm, growing vegetables for the market, and had put up the barn first, before they could afford to build a house. A friend recalls a telling episode from the young Leo's upbringing. "When he was a little boy his father told him that the only thing worthwhile in this whole world was what you accomplished at work, and that if you were not working you were lazy, which was a sin. So Leo judged himself and everyone else by that . . . and himself hardest of all."

Although Leo went on to study accountancy and worked in the accounts sections of the state highway department and a tyre distribution company, his hobby was always electronics, and in his 20s he built amplifiers and PA systems for use at public events such as sports and religious gatherings.

FENDER RADIO SERVICE

In about 1939 Leo opened a radio and record store in Fullerton, having lost his accounting job earlier in that decade of the Depression. The Fender Radio Service, as he called the new retail and repair shop, seemed a natural step for the ambitious, newly-married 30 year-old to take, and Leo advertised his wares and services as "electrical appliances, phonograph records, musical instruments & repairs, public address systems, sheet music".

Lap-steel guitar playing, often called Hawaiian guitar, had been fashionable in the United States since the 1920s and was still tremendously popular at the time Leo opened his new store. The lap-steel guitar is played horizontally on the player's lap, and the strings are stopped with a sliding steel bar held in the player's non-picking hand. Because of their popularity, lap-steels were the first guitars to 'go electric' in the 1930s. Several innovative companies such as Rickenbacker started experimenting with electro-magnetic pickups attached to guitars and connected to small amplifiers. The term 'Spanish' was used to identify the less popular 'normal', non-lap guitar.

Leo's new shop on South Spadra brought instant introductions to many local musicians and to people in the music and electronics businesses, and during the first few years he met several people who would prove very important to his future success. First of these was a professional violinist and lap-steel guitarist called Clayton Orr Kauffman, known to all as Doc.

The story goes that some time in the early 1940s Doc brought into Leo's shop an amp for repair, and the two got chatting. Doc had worked on electric guitar designs for another local company, Rickenbacker, and Leo had by this time already begun to look into the potential for electric guitars and to play around with pickup designs (a solid guitar built to test these early pickups is now in the collection of Roy Acuff's museum at Opryland, Nashville). Doc went to work for an aircraft company during World War II, but Leo and Doc still found time to get together, and the two incorrigible tinkerers came up with a design for a record-changer design good enough to net them $5000. Some of this money went into starting their shortlived company, K&F (Kauffman & Fender), and they began to produce electric lap-steel guitars and small amplifiers toward the end of 1945.

Doc later wrote: "We would go down to the store, and at the rear was a metal building that housed the guitar department and we would work till midnight." This description of a 'guitar department' is certainly optimistic – most people who saw the 'metal building' have described it as a tin shack hastily and cheaply assembled at the back of Leo's radio store. Doc continued: "I used to assemble all our instruments and string them up and play a few steel licks, and Leo used to say he could tell how production was coming along by counting the tunes I was playing."

Another significant person whom Leo started working with at this early stage was Don Randall, whom many view as a key contributor to the later success of the Fender company. Randall operated a small radio wholesale house selling parts and equipment, and one of his customers was the Fender Radio Service.

Leo had not served in World War II because of a childhood accident on his father's farm wagon which had cost him his right eye. Randall, who spent three years in the army, notes that Leo was able to expand his shop's trade in those war years. "During that period there weren't too many people about to do that kind of business," recalls Randall. "When I got out of the service I came back and started doing business with Leo again, selling parts and equipment." Randall was general manager of Radio & Television Equipment Co (R&TEC) in Santa Ana, some 15 miles south of Fullerton. R&TEC, owned by Francis Hall, became the exclusive distributor of Fender products in 1946 (a company called Pacific Music Supply also briefly acted as an outlet for some products). "By that time," Randall continues, "Leo and Doc Kauffman had split. It seems Doc was afraid to carry on with the business."

Leo was happy to work into the middle of the night at the tin shack making the K&F lap-steel guitars and amps, but apparently Doc wasn't so keen about these long hours locked away from the world. Leo told BAM magazine: "It cost a lot of money to get into large scale production, and the 1930s depression was still fresh in Kauffman's mind, so he didn't want to get involved. He had a ranch or farm in Oklahoma, and he was afraid if we got over-extended on credit he might lose it. He thought he'd better pull out while he had a full skin, so in February of '46 he left it all with me."

According to one colleague, Doc was asked later if he was resentful at having sold out, given the subsequent success of Fender. "And Doc said no, he was never sore, because Leo would have killed him before he got through with it anyway! Doc liked to spend time with his family, he didn't like staying down the shack till 10 or 11 at night, seven days a week. Anyone that worked with Leo had a hard time not over-working, because he expected you to be on call all hours."

FENDER ELECTRIC INSTRUMENTS

So Leo and Doc parted, and in 1946 Leo formed the Fender Electric Instrument Co, continuing to make lap steels and amps as he had with K&F, but gradually developing new products. Leo also expanded into larger premises on nearby South Pomona Avenue in Fullerton, separate from the radio store. The new property was described by one observer as "two plain, steel buildings, not very handsome" and another Fender associate remembers that the Pomona buildings did not have their own toilets. Consequently, Fender workers had to cross the nearby railroad tracks to use the rest-rooms in the Santa Fe depot.

Fender ad 1950 *(right)*
From a music trade journal, this shows the Fender-equipped Spade Cooley Band complete with an early Esquire.

Telecaster 1952 *(right)*
This guitar – another well-used and worn example – is from the second year of Telecaster production, with the same cosmetics as the original Broadcaster. Controls, too, appear the same, but around this time Fender changed the circuitry of the Telecaster. In the original system the second rotary control acted as a blender between the pickups; the new layout replaced this with a conventional tone control.

Esquire 1951 *(above)*
After a false start the Esquire reappeared in 1950, this time with Fender's new adjustable truss-rod. It was offered in single-pickup format only, and apart from this difference the Esquire was essentially identical to the Telecaster. However, the three-way selector functioned as a preset tone control or bypass switch, offering wide versatility from a one-pickup instrument. Perhaps surprisingly, this model stayed in the range for 20 years.

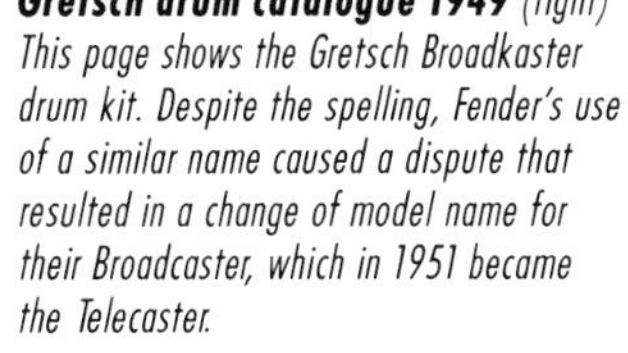

Gretsch drum catalogue 1949 *(right)*
This page shows the Gretsch Broadkaster drum kit. Despite the spelling, Fender's use of a similar name caused a dispute that resulted in a change of model name for their Broadcaster, which in 1951 became the Telecaster.

Broadcaster 1950 *(above)*
The first commercial outing for the now familiar Telecaster shape, the Broadcaster was produced only during 1950. The original see-through blond finish of this example has darkened in the ensuing 40 years, and the wear on the fingerboard is evidence of a well-used guitar. As is so often the case the metal cover over the bridge-plate has gone missing. It would now be almost impossible to find an original Broadcaster in pristine condition, but even careworn examples command high sums because of their historical significance.

Fender ad early 1950s *(above)*

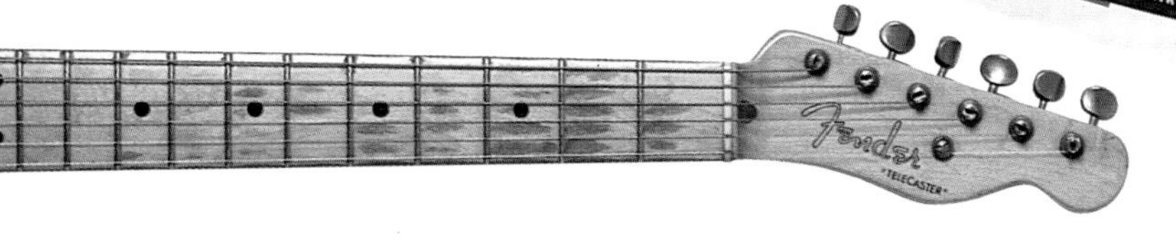

Fender catalogue early 1950s *(above)*
The cover shows a number of the company's endorsers of the period proudly displaying their 'fine electric instruments' from Fullerton.

Eventually one rather old employee couldn't make the treacherous trans-railroad journey, and the next day Leo had no choice but to hire a portable toilet.

Yet another important member of the growing Fender team, Dale Hyatt, had joined the company in January 1946. Hyatt later became a crucial member of the Fender sales team, but one of his early tasks, in late 1947 or early 1948, was to take over the radio store business because Leo was busy starting operations at the Pomona buildings.

Post-War Optimism

Leo was an introverted, hard-working man, prone to long hours and selfless application to the task in hand, happiest when by himself and drawing up designs for new projects. He had an idea that if there was a product on the market already, he could make it better and cheaper – and make a profit in the process. Now World War II was over there was a general feeling that a fresh start was possible, and one of the great processes that many American businessmen were exploiting to achieve such aims was mass-production. Leo's particular application of this technique to guitar manufacture was to be his master-stroke, but in these early days he still needed outside expertise in the mass-production of parts. And so another piece of the jigsaw came into place.

Karl Olmsted and his partner Lymon Race left the services in 1947 and decided to start a much-needed tool-and-die company in Fullerton, making dies to stamp out metal parts of the customer's choice. "We were looking for work," explains Karl, "and Leo had reached the point where he needed dies made for production work. They had been making parts by hand, cutting out the metal any way they could. But he was getting to the point where they wanted to make several of each thing." Race & Olmsted continued to make Fender's tooling and most metal parts for over 30 years. "As it progressed, so we progressed to more complicated, sophisticated, high-production tooling," Olmsted says.

Next to join Fender's company was George Fullerton, who was to become what one colleague describes as "Leo's faithful workhorse". The two had met at one of the outdoor events to which Leo was still supplying PA systems, and the young George, who remembers his activities at the time as "going to school, playing music, repairing radios and delivering furniture", began to help Leo with the PA events. Gradually, George's radio repair turned to fixing amps and lap-steels, and he started working at Pomona in February 1948. "It was only a small place then," he remembers, "only two or three people, a couple of girls."

Despite the popularity of the electric lap-steels that the Fender company were making, Leo wanted to produce a solid electric guitar of normal shape and playing style: 'electric Spanish', as the avant-garde instrument was called at the time. Leo was not entirely alone in this desire. During the 1930s some guitar makers in the United States, most notably Rickenbacker and National in California, Epiphone in New York, and Gibson in Michigan, had taken the original step of building electric pickups and controls into traditional hollow-bodied archtop guitars. Demand was rising from dance-band guitarists who found themselves failing to compete with the volume of the rest of the band. But these early experimental electric-acoustic guitars were only partially successful from a technical standpoint and still to become a great commercial sensation.

Other guitar makers, musicians and engineers in America were wondering about the possibility of a solid-bodied instrument. Such a design would curtail the annoying feedback often produced by amplified hollow-bodied guitars, at the same time reducing the body's interference with the guitar's tone and thus more accurately reproducing and sustaining the sound of the strings. Rickenbacker had launched a solid Bakelite-bodied electric guitar in the mid-1930s, while towards 1940 guitarist Les Paul built a test-bed electric guitar on his workbench in New Jersey, co-opting parts from a variety of instruments and mounting them on a solid central block of pine.

In Downey, California, about 15 miles to the west of Fender's operation in Fullerton, Paul Bigsby had a small workshop where he spent a good deal of time fixing motorcycles and, later, making some fine pedal-steel guitars and vibrato units. He also ventured into the solid-bodied electric guitar field, hand-building a limited number of distinctive instruments. It's difficult to judge whether the design of Fender's first solid-bodied electric guitar was influenced very much by Bigsby's earlier instruments. George Fullerton says that he and Leo knew Paul Bigsby and had seen country musician Merle Travis playing a Bigsby guitar. Dale Hyatt, however, says, "I can't really say there was any truth that Leo copied Paul Bigsby, they just both made something at the same time."

What Fender made was the instrument which we now know as the Fender **Telecaster**, effectively the world's first commercially successful solid-bodied electric guitar, and still very much alive today. The guitar, originally named the Fender **Esquire** or Fender **Broadcaster**, first went into production in 1950. This simple, effective instrument with its basic, single-cutaway solid slab of ash for a body and screwed-on fretted maple neck was geared to mass-production. It had a slanted pickup mounted into a steel bridge-plate carrying three adjustable bridge-saddles, and the body was finished in a yellowish colour known as 'blond'. Leo once said that this was influenced by the blond colour (natural finish) of some of the big-bodied jazz guitars made by companies such as Epiphone at the time.

Fender's new solid-bodied electric guitar was unadorned, straightforward, potent, and ahead of its time. As such it did not prove immediately easy to sell, as Don Randall of R&TEC found when he took some prototypes to a musical instrument trade show. "I just got laughed out of the place, it was called everything from a canoe paddle to the snow shovel." Dale Hyatt also had to struggle against a less than serious view of these new Fenders he was trying to sell, with one early potential customer in San Francisco offering to swap his son's electric train-set for a guitar.

Randall did have at least one useful meeting at the trade show, however, when Al Frost from National explained that the prototypes' lack of neck truss-rods would be likely to cause problems later for neck stability. Despite Leo's arguments to the contrary, this was later rectified by adding an adjustable truss-rod to the Fender guitar's neck.

Production of the instrument began at Pomona Avenue in early 1950, despite a cash-flow problem at Fender which for a few months endangered the company's future. One employee reports that there were times when it was hard to cash Fender cheques in Fullerton, especially if Leo's wife Esther was late in receiving her wages from the phone company. Fender also had to contend with the apparent reticence of music stores to stock the new guitar, and Fender's trade distributor was hesitant, as Dale Hyatt remembers. "R&TEC didn't want to take right off into the Spanish guitar business, didn't jump right on it as a money-maker. They were still expanding and building the market with the amplifiers and steels, and didn't think that the Spanish type guitar was going to be too big a success. So the first literature and advertising on the solid body guitar was done by Leo himself. We sold guitars directly out of the factory, I sold many of them on the bandstand myself, simply to keep bringing money in. Leo and George and I would go out on to the bandstands and contact the guitar players that would use them. That's how it came about."

The Original Esquire

Fender devotee Richard Smith has established a chronology for the three varieties of the early Fender electric solid, which were of the same basic design but bore different names. A very few one-pickup Esquire models without truss-rods were made in April 1950, with another tiny production run of two-pickup Esquires two months later. General production of the better-known single-pickup Esquire with truss-rod did not begin until January 1951.

Stratocaster 1957 *(left)*
An early example finished in a custom colour, a rare option for the time, and rarer still is the gold-plated hardware; the combination makes for a very special instrument. It was owned at one time by Homer Haynes.

Fender catalogue 1957/58 *(above)*
Three years into the Stratocaster's life, the front cover of this promotional leaflet includes a rather crude artist's impression of the outline of Fender's top solid.

Stratocaster 1959 *(above)*
This was one of the first Strats brought into the UK, specially imported by Cliff Richard for Shadows' guitarist Hank Marvin. It is now owned by another member of the group, Bruce Welch, and has been restored to original condition, with gold hardware on custom-colour body.

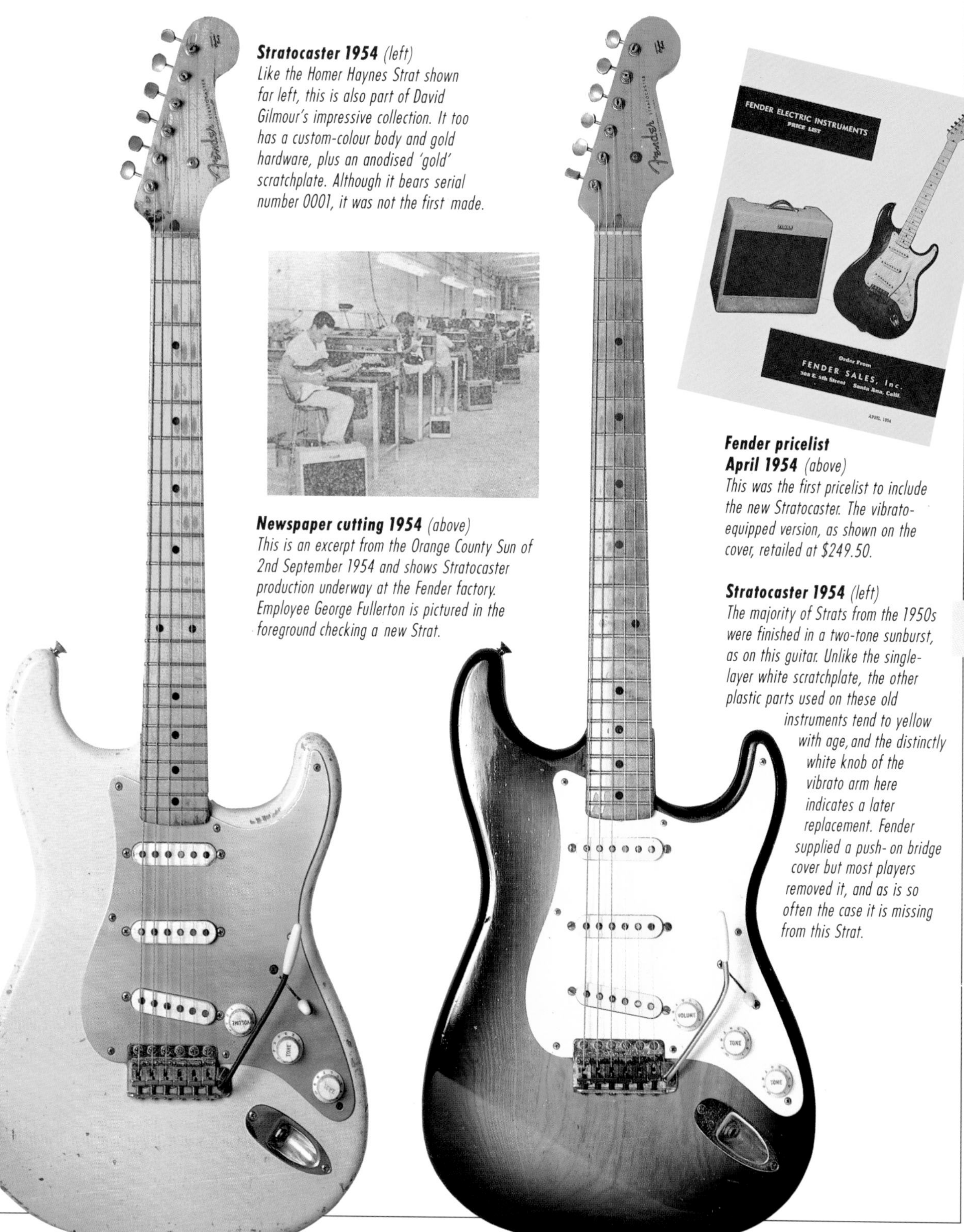

Stratocaster 1954 *(left)*
Like the Homer Haynes Strat shown far left, this is also part of David Gilmour's impressive collection. It too has a custom-colour body and gold hardware, plus an anodised 'gold' scratchplate. Although it bears serial number 0001, it was not the first made.

Newspaper cutting 1954 *(above)*
This is an excerpt from the Orange County Sun of 2nd September 1954 and shows Stratocaster production underway at the Fender factory. Employee George Fullerton is pictured in the foreground checking a new Strat.

Fender pricelist April 1954 *(above)*
This was the first pricelist to include the new Stratocaster. The vibrato-equipped version, as shown on the cover, retailed at $249.50.

Stratocaster 1954 *(left)*
The majority of Strats from the 1950s were finished in a two-tone sunburst, as on this guitar. Unlike the single-layer white scratchplate, the other plastic parts used on these old instruments tend to yellow with age, and the distinctly white knob of the vibrato arm here indicates a later replacement. Fender supplied a push-on bridge cover but most players removed it, and as is so often the case it is missing from this Strat.

But back in November 1950, a truss-rod was added to the two-pickup model, its name was changed to Broadcaster, and the retail price was fixed at $169.95. The Broadcaster was really the first Fender solid electric to be made and sold in any reasonable quantity, as confirmed by Leo who told Guitar Player magazine in 1984: "The single- and double-pickup guitars overlapped . . . but the Broadcaster was the first one we built," in other words, we can presume, *built in significant numbers.* The Fender Broadcaster is thus the historically significant guitar.

Use of the Broadcaster name was shortlived, halted in early 1951 after Gretsch, a large New York-based instrument manufacturer, indicated their prior use of the name 'Broadkaster' on various drum products. Gretsch had already stopped another drum company, Slingerland, from using the name, and evidently were sufficiently troubled by Fender's guitar to block that use too. Fender complied, as Dale Hyatt explains: "There was a camaraderie between the manufacturers in the early days and no-one was trying to beat the other to a patent or anything like that. So Gretsch just pointed it out and we agreed to do it."

This is echoed in Don Randall's letter of 21st February 1951 to his Fender salesmen, outlining the necessity of a change of name. He told them that Gretsch had advised Fender of the infringement of a copyrighted name, writing: "We have checked this and are inclined to agree that they are fair in their request. Consequently, it behooves us to find a new name . . . if any of you have a good name in mind I would welcome hearing from you immediately."

At first, from the February until around August 1951, Fender simply used up their 'Fender Broadcaster' transfers on the guitar's headstock by cutting off the 'Broadcaster' and leaving just the 'Fender' logo; these no-name guitars are known among collectors today as 'No-casters'.

The new name finally decided upon for the Fender solid electric was 'Telecaster', coined by Don Randall (who came up with all the well-known Fender model names, with the exception of 'Precision Bass' which was Leo's idea). 'Telecaster' was certainly an appropriate-sounding name, fresh from the new age of television and telecasts. Leo himself was well aware of the drawing power of TV, as George Fullerton remembers: "When television was brand new, Leo's store was probably the only place in town that had televisions, and he used to have one that he'd put in the window facing out into the street, speaker outside. At night there'd be a crowd of people around watching wrestling or whatever was on. Sometimes it would be cold and foggy, but there'd still be this crowd of people."

The Telecaster name was on headstocks by April 1951, and at last Fender's premier solid had a permanent name.

At Fender, practicality and function ruled. There was no hand carving of selected timbers as one would find in the workshops of established archtop guitar makers. With the Telecaster,Fender made the electric guitar into a factory product, stripped down to its essential elements, built up from easily assembled parts, and produced at an affordable price. Fender's methods made for easier, more consistent production – and a different sound. Not for Fender the fat, Gibson-style jazz tone, but a clearer, sustained sound, something like a cross between a clean acoustic guitar and a cutting electric lap-steel.

Electric Endorsement

One of the earliest players to appreciate this new sound was Jimmy Bryant, best known for his staggering guitar instrumental duets with pedal-steel virtuoso Speedy West. George Fullerton remembers Bryant's early encounter with Fender's new solid electric. Leo and George had taken an early Broadcaster out to a Los Angeles nightclub and Bryant took a look at this strange new guitar, picked it up, and started playing. "He got to do a lot of neat things on this guitar, and pretty soon all these people who'd been dancing were crowding around listening to what he was doing, and it wasn't long before the whole band was standing around too," says Fullerton.

"He was the centre of attention. Jimmy played things on guitar that nobody could play. And course this was an electric with low action – and with that cutaway he could go right down the neck.

"So naturally we put one in his hand, and this was like starting a prairie fire. Pretty soon we couldn't make enough of those guitars. That wasn't the only reason, but it was a lot of it, because Jimmy was on television shows, personal appearances, and everybody wanted a guitar like Jimmy Bryant's. That was one of the starting points of that guitar."

Fullerton says that Fender guitars were aimed at the working musician. "You think of a cowboy and you think of Roy Rogers, Gene Autry, the big silver screen and cowboys in their fancy hats and shirts and boots and their shiny gold-plated guns. But did you ever see a working cowboy? He's dirty and got rough boots on and heavy leather on his pants. So we kind of looked at guitar players as being working cowboys. If you're going to go out on stage and it's a personal appearance and you're a top notch entertainer, well, you might want a flashy guitar and flashy clothing. But you're not a working musician, and Fender doesn't fit with your dress code."

Fender Sales Inc.

Business began to pick up for the Fender company as news of the Telecaster spread among working musicians, and as the five R&TEC salesmen (Charlie Hayes, Don Patton, Dave Driver, Mike Cole and Art Bates) helped persuade guitar dealers to stock the instrument. In 1953 Fender's existing sales set-up with R&TEC was re-organised into the new Fender Sales company, based like R&TEC in Santa Ana and with four business partners: Leo, Don Randall, Francis Hall and Charlie Hayes (the latter three coming from R&TEC). Hayes was killed in a road accident in 1955 (Dale Hyatt took over his sales patch, Fender's radio store having closed in 1951), while Hall bought the Rickenbacker company. So in 1955 Fender Sales became a partnership between Leo and Don Randall, though it was Randall who actually ran this pivotal part of the Fender business. As Dale Hyatt says, "You can make the finest guitar in the world, but if you don't sell the first one you're not going to get the chance to make another one."

So the sales side of Fender was in capable hands. Another important addition to the Fender team occurred in 1953 when steel guitarist Freddie Tavares, best known for his swooping steel intro over the titles of the Looney Tunes cartoons, joined the Californian guitar maker, principally to help Leo design new products. Tavares told Guitar Player in 1979: "When it was just Leo and I we did what we pleased. In other words Leo did what he pleased, and I was just his assistant." A colleague describes Freddie, who died in 1990, as "one of the best musicians I have ever known, and just as good at engineering. A very talented man."

Also in 1953 the manufacturing side of the company acquired three new buildings on a 3.5 acre plot at South Raymond Avenue and Valencia Drive in Fullerton. Clearly expansion of Fender's product lines was imminent: a trade magazine reported in 1953 that with these changes the company "hoped that production will be upped by almost 100 per cent in the next few months".

But first their rather haphazard production methods had to be organised more efficiently. This job fell into the very capable hands of a newcomer, Forrest White, who had worked as an industrial engineer at an aircraft firm in Akron, Ohio. On a business trip to Los Angeles in 1944 he'd fallen in love with the area and became determined to move there. White had built several guitars in his spare time, including an early solid-body electric ("way before Leo did," he emphasises).

White's opportunity to move out west occurred in 1951 when the engineer was hired by a company in Riverside, California. He'd already met Leo a few times when, in spring 1954, the two had lunch and Leo asked Forrest if he'd be interested in helping him sort out some 'management problems' at Fender. White remembers their conversation. "Freddie Tavares had told Leo that the company was ready to go down the drain, it was that bad.

Fender catalogue 1958/59
(right)
This was one of Fender's first full-colour catalogue covers, impressively designed to represent the complete range at that time – although the then-new Jazzmaster does not appear.

Jazzmaster 1959 *(below)*
Launched in 1958 this became Fender's top-of-the-line model and featured an enlarged headstock design. It had a distinctive body with offset waist (one of Fender's many patents) and other 'Fender firsts' included the separate rhythm circuit and floating vibrato unit. The guitar shown has a custom-colour body with anodised 'gold' scratchplate.

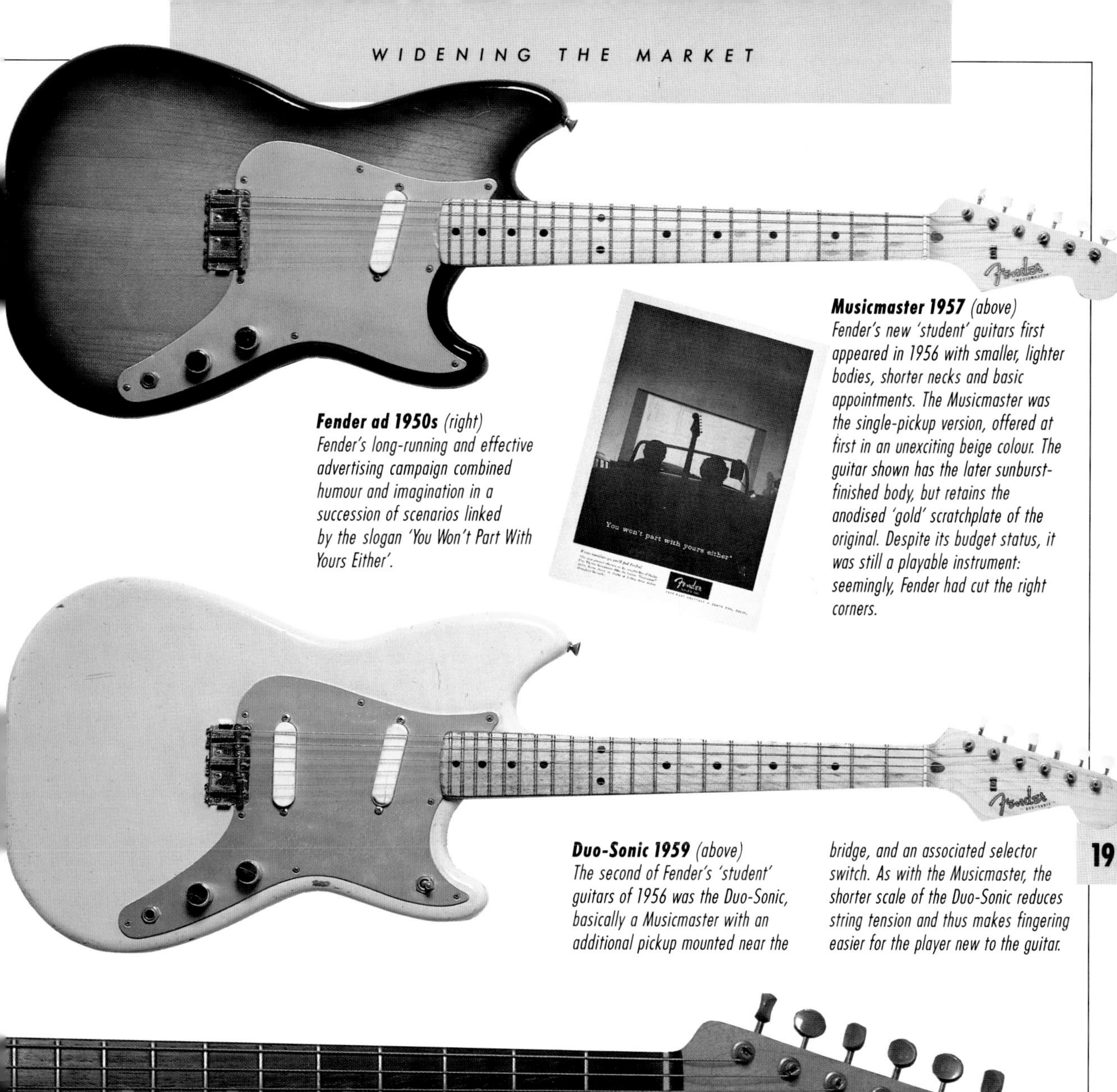

Musicmaster 1957 *(above)*
Fender's new 'student' guitars first appeared in 1956 with smaller, lighter bodies, shorter necks and basic appointments. The Musicmaster was the single-pickup version, offered at first in an unexciting beige colour. The guitar shown has the later sunburst-finished body, but retains the anodised 'gold' scratchplate of the original. Despite its budget status, it was still a playable instrument: seemingly, Fender had cut the right corners.

Fender ad 1950s *(right)*
Fender's long-running and effective advertising campaign combined humour and imagination in a succession of scenarios linked by the slogan 'You Won't Part With Yours Either'.

Duo-Sonic 1959 *(above)*
The second of Fender's 'student' guitars of 1956 was the Duo-Sonic, basically a Musicmaster with an additional pickup mounted near the bridge, and an associated selector switch. As with the Musicmaster, the shorter scale of the Duo-Sonic reduces string tension and thus makes fingering easier for the player new to the guitar.

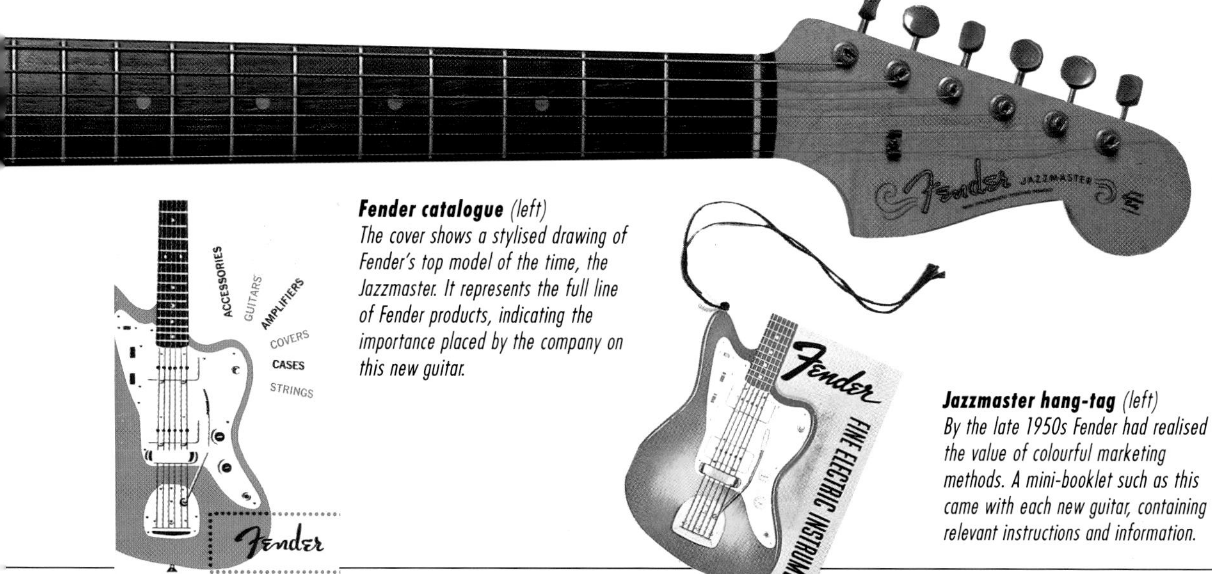

Fender catalogue *(left)*
The cover shows a stylised drawing of Fender's top model of the time, the Jazzmaster. It represents the full line of Fender products, indicating the importance placed by the company on this new guitar.

Jazzmaster hang-tag *(left)*
By the late 1950s Fender had realised the value of colourful marketing methods. A mini-booklet such as this came with each new guitar, containing relevant instructions and information.

He had no credit whatsoever, had to pay cash buying any material and so on. Some of the employees' cheques were bouncing. Freddie had said that Leo didn't have anyone in the plant that could do what needed to be done. So it just so happened that my timing was right."

Karl Olmsted of Race & Olmsted, Fender's tool-and-die maker, also remembers how close Fender came to going broke at the time. "He tried to buy us with stock, to get out of paying our bills, and like idiots we didn't take the bait," laughs Olmsted. "I'm not sorry that I didn't, because I'm not sure that I could have worked for Leo day in, day out. At least we had the advantage of occasionally being able to say Leo, this is all I can take, and stepping back. As good as the relationship was, once in a while you had to do that -and I couldn't have done that if they'd taken us over. We just gave him credit and credit and credit, practically to the point where we couldn't make our pay-roll and bills and everything else. If this guitar craze hadn't taken off, he wouldn't have made it. So genius has to have some luck – and he had both."

FACTORY ORGANISATION

Meanwhile, Leo took an intrigued Forrest White to look at Fender's set-up at the new South Raymond buildings. "And it was a mess," White remembers. "There was no planning whatsoever, because Leo was not an engineer, he was an accountant. Things had just been set down any place. Man, everything was just so mixed up, you can't believe it. There was no planning whatsoever because in all fairness to him he didn't have any experience in things like that."

So White agreed to come in and work for Leo. "But I said it depends on one thing. If I can have a free hand to do what I know has to be done, fine. Otherwise I'm not interested. He gave me that free hand. When I stepped in, from that point on I ran the company. He stayed in design, but I ran it."

One of the most important aspects of production which White clarified was an incentive scheme tied to quality control, where assemblers on the production line did not accept a product from the previous stage unless they were happy that it was perfect – effectively making each operator an inspector. "The reason for that," White explains, "was that if it had to be re-worked, it was on their own time. If someone loused up, hey, once they accepted it, then it's their problem. But as long as they turned out good production that passed, they made good money, darned good money."

Now Leo had able men – Forrest White and Don Randall – poised at the head of the production and sales halves of the Fender company. He had a new factory, and a small but growing reputation. All he needed now, it seemed, were more new products. And so the stylish Fender **Stratocaster** was born, epitome of the tailfin-flash American design of the 1950s – and almost universally abbreviated among players as 'the Strat'.

THE STRATOCASTER: 'AN UPGRADE'

Don Randall is typically unsentimental in his recollection of the birth. "You know, the Esquire and Telecaster are pretty ugly guitars when it comes right down to it. In the days of Gibsons and things with bound necks and purfling they were plain vanilla, but we thought they were beautiful because we were making money with them. And so we needed a fancier guitar, an upgrade guitar – the Stratocaster."

Leo was listening hard to players' comments about the 'plain vanilla' Tele and Esquire, and during the early 1950s he and Freddie Tavares began to formulate the guitar that would become the Stratocaster. Some players complained that the sharp edge on the Telecaster was uncomfortable, so the team began to toy with body contours.

Among the dissenting voices were those of western swing guitarist Bill Carson and entertainer Rex Galleon. Carson had moved to California in 1951 and sought out Leo Fender because he'd tried a Broadcaster, loved its feel, and wanted a guitar made. He was given a Telecaster and amp but, as he didn't have enough to buy them outright, agreed to pay $18 a month and act as musical guinea-pig for new products. He did this for a number of years, mainly lugging test-bed amps along to his club gigs, often turning around to see Leo Fender ("oblivious of musicians, audience, club management and disruption generally") busily changing the amp settings in mid-song.

But as far as his Telecaster went, Carson gradually came to the conclusion that he wanted something more. Today, he recalls the basic specs of his 1950s dream guitar as follows: "Six bridges that would adjust vertically and horizontally, four pickups, the guitar should fit like a good shirt, with body contours, and stay balanced at all times, have a Bigsby-style headstock, and a vibrato that would not only come back to exact string pitch after you'd sharped or flatted it, but that would also sharp or flat half a tone at least and hold the chord. And that was tough to do, according to Leo."

It's clear that some of these ideas ended up being incorporated into the Stratocaster, eventually launched during 1954. Carson's four pickups didn't quite make it but the new Fender guitar was nonetheless the first solid electric with three (Gibson's electric-acoustic ES5, introduced five years earlier, had been the overall first). Freddie Tavares told Guitar Player in 1979: "Leo would say . . . let's put in three pickups. Two is good, but three will kill them!"

Trouble With The Vibrato

The Strat also featured a newly-designed built-in vibrato unit (erroneously called a 'tremolo' by Fender and many others since) to provide pitch-bending and shimmering chordal effects for the player. The unit ("Leo's pride and joy," says Randall) gave the Fender team severe headaches in its development stages. One version was completely scrapped, along with several thousand dollars' worth of tooling. Fender's tool-maker Karl Olmsted remembers, for example, the trouble taken over the individual bridge-saddles. "We had a heck of a time getting this little thing developed so it was practical to stamp out and mass-produce, and that worked the way Leo wanted it to. There was no way to make cheaply the original ones they wanted, they would have had to machine them out. So something that looks quite simple actually wound up being quite a development."

The eventual result of all this work was the first self-contained vibrato unit: adjustable bridge, tailpiece and vibrato system all in one. Not a simple mechanism for the time, but a reasonably effective one. It followed the Fender principle of taking an existing product (such as the Bigsby vibrato) and improving on it. This was typical of Fender's constant consideration of a musician's requirement and consequent application of a mass-producer's solution.

The Strat came with a radically sleek, solid body contoured for the player's comfort and finished in a yellow-to-black sunburst finish. Even the jack socket mounting was new, recessed in a stylish plate on the body face. And the headstock? Looking at it side by side with the Bigsby guitar, one would have to conclude that there must be some influence from that earlier instrument. But as a whole the Fender Stratocaster looked like no other guitar around – and in some ways seemed to owe more to contemporary automobile design than traditional guitar forms, especially in the flowing, sensual curves of that beautifully proportioned, timeless body. The new-style scratchplate complemented the lines perfectly, and the overall impression was of a guitar where all the components suited one another perfectly. It's not surprising, therefore, that the Strat is still made today, nearly 40 years after its birth in the Fender company's functional buildings in Fullerton, California. The exemplary Fender Stratocaster has become the most popular, the most copied, the most desired, and very probably the most played solid electric guitar ever.

However, in the beginning it wasn't quite such a world-beater, as salesman Dale Hyatt recollects. "Let me tell you, the dealers didn't just grab it, they didn't take 'em away from you. The vibrato system was something that was very difficult for most of them to get used to,

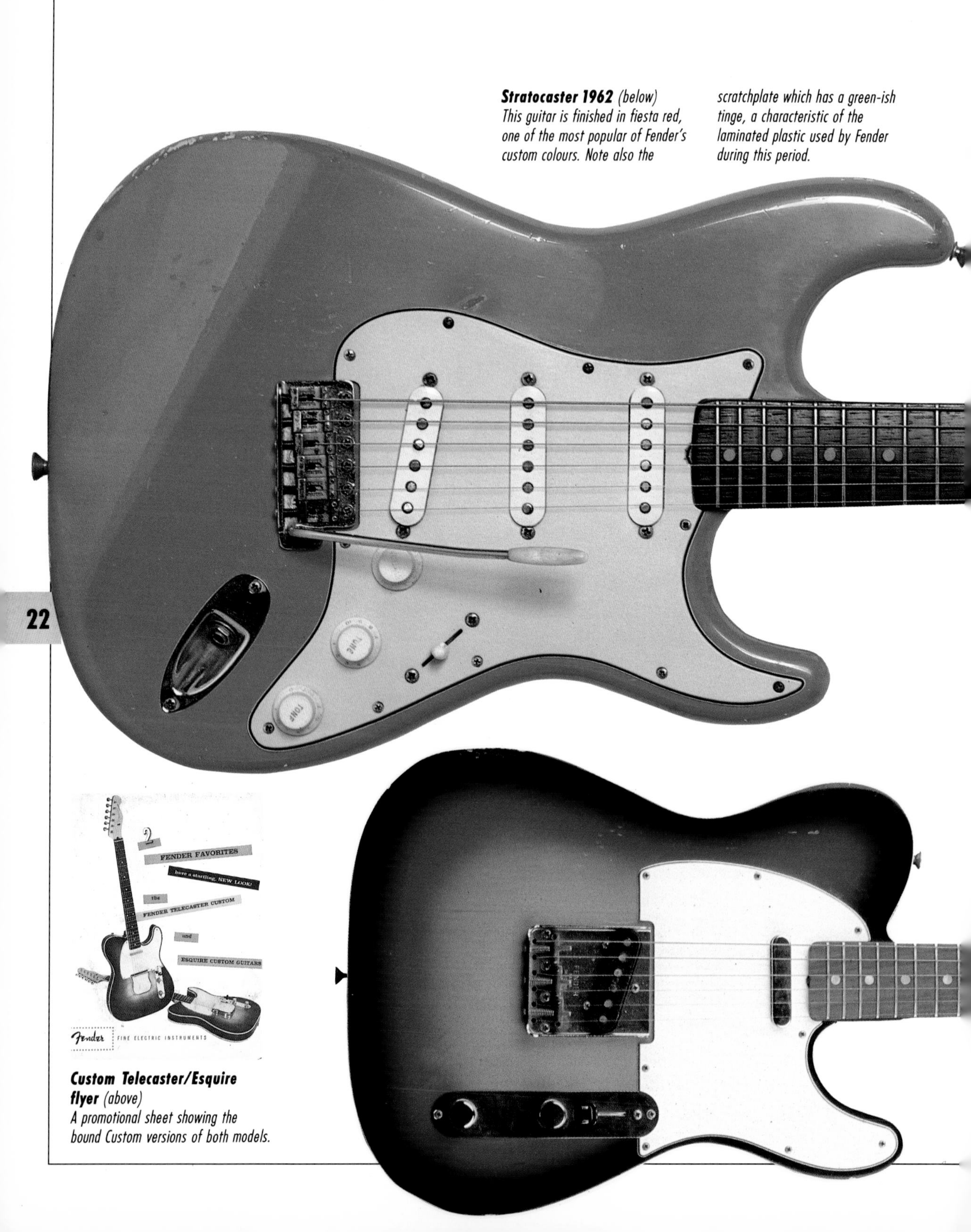

Stratocaster 1962 *(below)*
This guitar is finished in fiesta red, one of the most popular of Fender's custom colours. Note also the scratchplate which has a green-ish tinge, a characteristic of the laminated plastic used by Fender during this period.

Custom Telecaster/Esquire flyer *(above)*
A promotional sheet showing the bound Custom versions of both models.

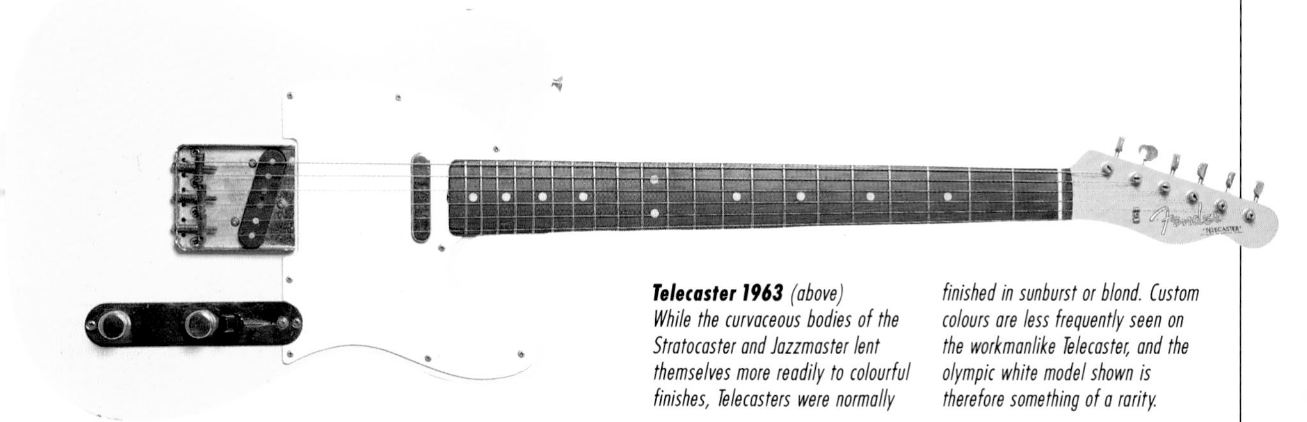

Telecaster 1963 *(above)*
While the curvaceous bodies of the Stratocaster and Jazzmaster lent themselves more readily to colourful finishes, Telecasters were normally finished in sunburst or blond. Custom colours are less frequently seen on the workmanlike Telecaster, and the olympic white model shown is therefore something of a rarity.

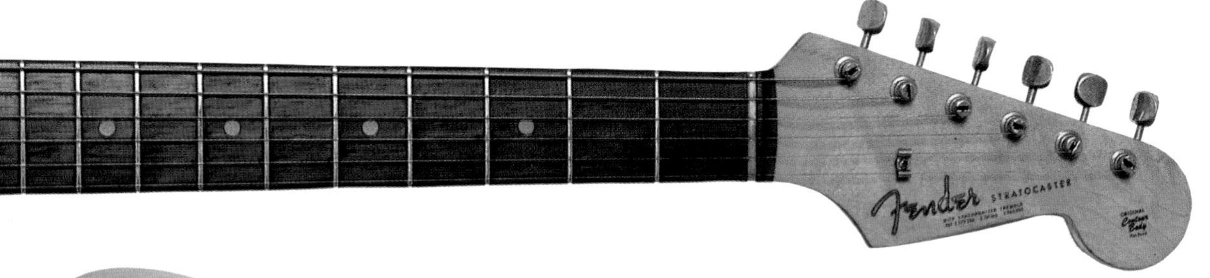

Stratocaster 1965 *(below)*
This ice blue Strat has a scratchplate made of the later laminated material, lacking the earlier green-ish tinge.

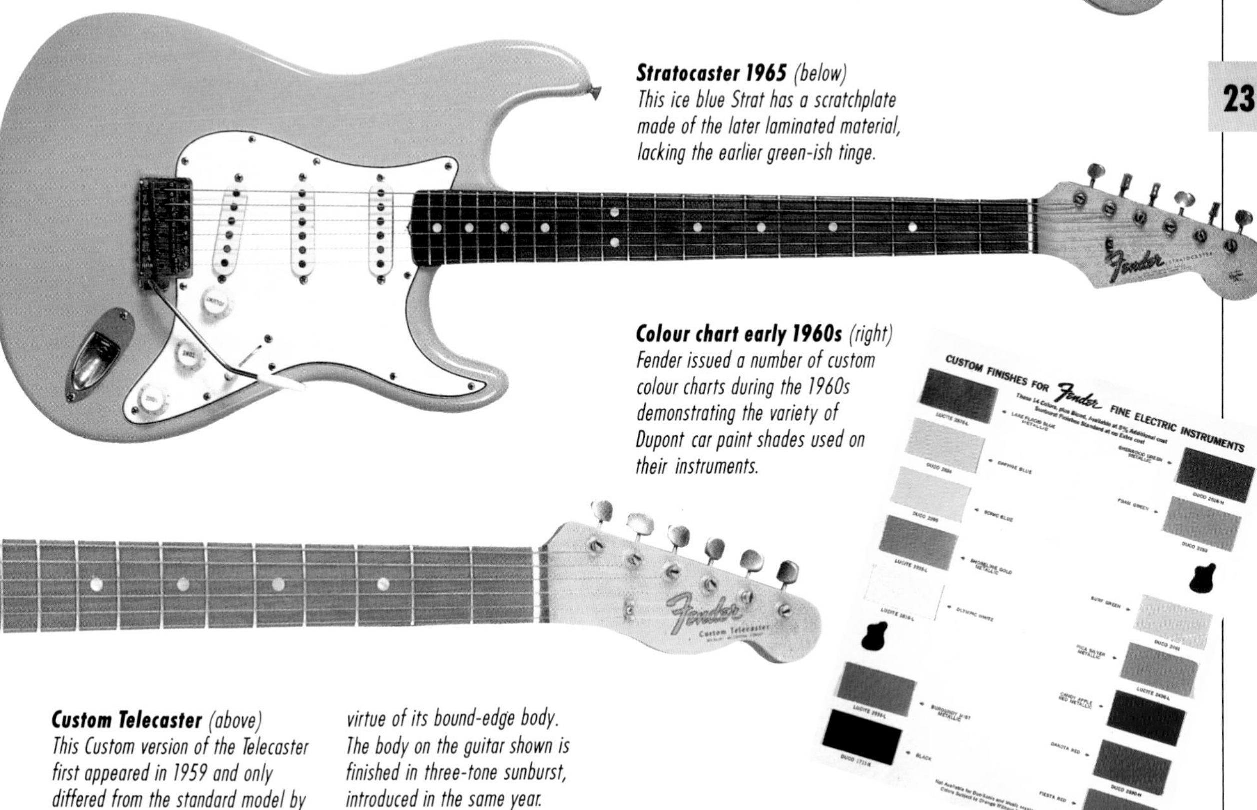

Colour chart early 1960s *(right)*
Fender issued a number of custom colour charts during the 1960s demonstrating the variety of Dupont car paint shades used on their instruments.

Custom Telecaster *(above)*
This Custom version of the Telecaster first appeared in 1959 and only differed from the standard model by virtue of its bound-edge body. The body on the guitar shown is finished in three-tone sunburst, introduced in the same year.

they said it'll never work, who needs it? You can bend the neck to do this kind of thing. But it caught on, nevertheless. It forced the musician to create a brand new wave of sound, a different style of playing. After rock'n'roll started, of course all these dealers were teaching the electric Spanish guitar . . . "

Which led Fender to introduce in 1956 a pair of new 'student' electrics, with 22.5in scale-length as opposed to Fender's customary 25.5in scale. These "three-quarter size" guitars – the one-pickup **Musicmaster** and two-pickup **Duo-Sonic** - were described in the company's literature as being "ideal for students and adults with small hands". They were designed for players on a tight budget, for those starting out on electric guitar. The two guitars certainly looked cheaper than Fender's Strat, Tele and Esquire – and indeed they sat at the bottom of Fender's pricelist (in February 1957, for example, the Strat with vibrato listed at $274.50, the Tele at $199.50, Esquire at $164.50, Duo-Sonic at $149.50, and the Musicmaster at $119.50).

Anodised Agonies

One feature of the Duo-Sonic and Musicmaster which seemed attractive was what Fender called their 'gold-finished pickguards'. These were in fact made from gold-coloured anodised aluminium, and the metal provided excellent electrical shielding, meaning less extraneous noise. The trouble was that the electrolytic anodised 'skin' wore through quite quickly to the aluminium, leaving unsightly grey patches.

As Forrest White puts it, "I said Leo don't do that, you'll wear through the anodised part and it'll look like the very devil. Looked nice to begin with, but my god, after the guy played it for a while, first thing you know you're wearing through the doggone deal. So that was a catastrophe." Realising their mistake, Fender dropped the idea after a couple of years.

Also around 1957 Fender began officially to offer some guitars with optional gold-plated hardware. "That was my idea," remembers Don Randall. "The White Falcon had come out from Gretsch, and we couldn't be outdone. Wasn't a very good move, actually. It was very hard to keep the gold to stay on. We found ourselves having to apologise and do it over." George Fullerton also recalls the difficulties such luxury caused: "Whatever was on your hands – sweat, dirt, acid, alcohol – had a tendency to eat through the gold-plating pretty fast. Wasn't long before it looked bad. So we didn't feel that was a good advertisement for the musician or the company or anybody else. So we resisted somewhat making gold finish instruments."

The Jazzmaster: 'Even Better'

For their next guitar Fender moved decidedly up-market. The **Jazzmaster** first appeared on Fender's pricelists in 1958, and at $329 was some $50 more expensive than the Strat. At that sort of price Fender could not resist tagging their new Jazzmaster "America's finest electric guitar . . . unequalled in performance and design features". Freddie Tavares, again responsible for some of the design input, told Guitar Player in 1979: "When we built the Stratocaster we thought that was the world's greatest guitar. Then we said let's make something even better, so we built the Jazzmaster."

Immediately striking to the guitarist of 1958 was the Jazzmaster's unusual offset-waist body shape and, for the first time on a Fender, a separate rosewood fingerboard glued to the customary maple neck. The vibrato system was new, too, with a 'lock-off' facility aimed at preventing tuning problems if a string should break.

The controls were certainly elaborate for the time. A small slide-switch selected between two individual circuits enabling the player to preset rhythm and lead sounds. This dual-circuit idea was adapted from a layout that Forrest White had designed way back in the 1940s when he built guitars as a hobby. White had put a switch into his guitar to flip between preset rhythm and lead tones. "Later, I said to Leo what you need is a guitar where you can preset the rhythm and lead. Leo didn't play guitar, he couldn't even tune a guitar, so he didn't think this was important. [Guitarist] Alvino Rey came in the plant one day, and I said how would you like not to have to mess around with the controls, just flip a switch? He says, can that be done? I says well sure, I already did it. So Leo brought the Jazzmaster out, and that instrument was the first guitar where you could switch between rhythm and lead."

The sound of the Jazzmaster was richer and warmer than players were used to from Fender. Indeed 'Jazzmaster' was in this respect an apposite choice of name, for there was some appeal to jazz players in its tone, even if the instrument did turn up more frequently in the hands of pop players. But Forrest White certainly remembers its jazz associations: "Leo was trying to get more of a jazz sound than the high, piercing Telecaster sound."

All in all, the Jazzmaster was a distinct change for Fender, and constituted a real effort to extend the scope and appeal of their guitar line. Ironically, and despite significant early success, this has been partly responsible for the guitar's lack of long-term popularity relative to the Strat and Tele, mainly as a result of players' dissatisfaction with the guitar's looks and sounds.

Don Randall seems especially harsh in his recollection. "It never met with very much favour because those big, wide, flat pickups were not shielded, so you'd come on stage in Las Vegas among all the wires and cables and you picked up too much hum and noise from the lights, static and all. So it was never very effective as an instrument."

Fashionable Clapton

Despite that retrospective judgement, the Jazzmaster remained near the top of the Fender pricelist until withdrawn around 1980. Five years later American guitar dealer George Gruhn wrote in Guitar Player magazine an intriguing postscript on the Jazzmaster and its place among the devious excursions of guitar fashion. "In about 1970 Eric Clapton began buying and playing Clapton bought quite a few Strats from me during this period and when he asked one day that I find a good Jazzmaster for him I had hopes that his use of the model would do comparable things for its collectability. However, circumstances intervened, Clapton decided he didn't want a Jazzmaster after all, and nothing further developed." Perhaps the Jazzmaster's fate might have been different had Mr Clapton's dice rolled another way?

Back at Fender in the late 1950s, a few cosmetic and production adjustments were being made to the company's electric guitars. As we've seen, the Jazzmaster was their first guitar with a rosewood fingerboard, adopted for other Fenders in 1959, and the company also altered the look of their sunburst guitars at this time by adding red, giving a yellow-to-red-to-black three-tone effect.

Custom Colours

Most Fender guitars of the 1950s came officially only in sunburst or varieties of the original 'blond'. Nonetheless a few guitars, specially ordered from the factory as one-offs, had been finished in solid colours. The rare surviving examples suggest that this practice started around 1954 (for example the greeny-blue '54 Strat shown on page 15), but very few players of the time seemed interested in slinging a coloured guitar around their shoulders, and Fender's main production remained in sunburst and blond instruments. The company's early production of special-colour guitars was certainly casual, often no doubt the understandable reaction of a small company to a customer walking through the door with dollars in his pocket and a strange whim in his heart. But this informal arrangement was given a rather more commercial footing in the company's sales literature of 1956 when 'player's choice' coloured guitars were noted as an option, at five per cent extra cost. By 1957 these were known as 'custom colors' in the catalogue and 'custom DuPont Ducco finishes' on the pricelist, still at five per cent on top of normal prices. Fender eventually came up with a defined list of their choice of available custom colours, and in the early 1960s when many more

Fender literature *(above)*
Fender's guitar tutor (top) and 1963/64 catalogue cover both featured the premier model of the time, the Jaguar.

Jaguar mute *(box below)*
This device proved unpopular and was often removed – as on the Jaguar illustrated (right).

Jaguar 1965 *(left)*
Launched in 1962 this superseded the Jazzmaster at the top of the Fender pricelist. It was based on the earlier instrument but with a shorter neck and more sophisticated controls.

Fender ad 1965 *(above)*
Another example from Fender's successful advertising campaign, this featuring the Electric XII in an unlikely situation.

Electric XII 1965 *(left)*
Unlike other companies who jumped on the electric 12-string bandwagon at this time, Fender's model was a purpose-built guitar – not just a six-string with a new neck. The XII shown is in candy apple red, with matching headstock face.

Fender Research & Development *(above)*
The R&D department in the mid 1960s, with work in progress on the Electric XII.

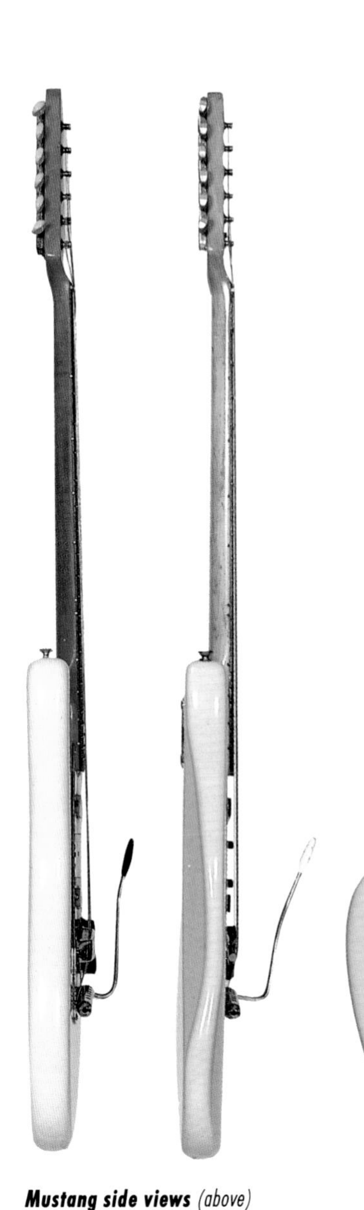

Fender catalogue 1965/66 *(above)*
Two prototypes of Fender's ill-fated Marauder guitar (left) with cunningly concealed pickups are featured on this page. Despite the model's appearance in this catalogue the Marauder never went into production.

Mustang 1971 *(left)*
Launched in 1964, the Mustang seemed to bridge the gap between Fender's 'student' models and the rest of their range, and was offered in two scale lengths. It echoed the Duo-Sonic theme, using two pickups but with more versatile circuitry. In reciprocal fashion, the Duo-Sonic's pickup layout and circuitry were updated in 1964 to match the new model. An added attraction of the Mustang was a newly-designed vibrato tailpiece, and until the mid-1970s the guitar came with pearl- or tortoiseshell-effect scratchplates.

Mustang side views *(above)*
These two guitars illustrate a variation in Mustang body styling. The early type (left) has a 'slab' body with no rear contouring, unlike the later version (right). In addition, the second version features Fender's offset-waist body design. These differences can also be seen on Duo-Sonic and Musicmaster guitars.

custom-colour Fenders were being made the company even issued colour-charts to demonstrate their range of around 14 varieties.

George Fullerton remembers going out to a local paint store around 1957 and having a bright red colour mixed up, which he took back to the factory to be applied to a guitar body. This experiment, he says, is what started Fender's defined custom colour range, which came to include shades with such evocative names as Lake Placid blue, shoreline gold and foam green, using the same bright DuPont paints seen on many glitzy automobile finishes of the period. "That first one became fiesta red," says Fullerton. "The DuPont company made that colour and you can buy it right across the counter. That should have been a patent, that fiesta red colour, but who knows at the time you do a thing? Meanwhile, the sales office and Don Randall laughed at it, said who in hell wants a coloured guitar, specially a red one . . . "

Don Randall has a different recollection of the genesis of Fender's custom colour range. "Gretsch had their Country Club which was green, the White Falcon which was white, and there were others. So it was just my idea to diversify and get another product on the market. They didn't sell as well as the traditional sunburst and blond colours." Forrest White backs up this notion that it was Fender Sales which implemented the custom colour scheme. "If Sales didn't place an order for something of a certain colour, we in production didn't build it. Sales picked out the colours they wanted and made up the brochure with the different colours."

Whatever the origins of Fender's custom colours, decades later the guitars bearing these original fiesta reds, sonic blues, burgundy mists and the like have proved very desirable among collectors, many of whom rate a custom colour Fender, especially an early one, as a prime catch.

CUSTOM TELES

Also around this time the Esquire and Telecaster were offered in visually different versions, the bound-body Custom models. Forrest White acquired some valuable advice on the process of binding from Fred Martin, head of the top American flat-top acoustic manufacturer Martin. "I said Fred, I'd like to put binding around a Telecaster but I don't know a darned thing about it. He showed me how they cut the binding material, bought in sheets and cut into strips, and what kind of adhesive to use. So I made three sparkle-finish bound Telecasters and a Precision Bass for [country musicians] Buck Owens and Don Rich, and those were the first Fenders with binding. Fender Sales saw what they looked like. They said would you like to make up a sunburst and a blond Telecaster and put white binding on?" Not surprisingly the white binding against sunburst looked the best, so that version was Fender's choice for the production **Custom** Teles and Esquires.

THE JAGUAR: 'ONE OF THE FINEST'

The next new guitar off Fender's production line was the **Jaguar** which first showed up in sales material during 1962 listed at around $30 more than the Jazzmaster ($379 for the basic sunburst Jaguar, for example). It used the same offset-waist body shape as the Jazzmaster, and also shared that guitar's separate bridge and vibrato unit, although the Jaguar had the addition of a spring-loaded string mute at the bridge. Fender rather optimistically believed that players would actually prefer the 'advantages' of a mechanical string mute to the natural method. They were wrong.

There were some notable differences between the Jaguar and Jazzmaster. Visually, the Jag had distinctive chrome control plates, and was the first Fender with 22 frets. Its 24in scale-length was shorter than the Fender norm of 25.5in, and it was offered in four neck widths, one a size narrower and two wider than normal (coded alongside the date on the neck-end stamp as A, B, C or D, from narrowest to widest). These neck options were also offered from 1962 on the Jazzmaster and Strat. From around 1960 Fender had begun using a modernised 'chunky' Fender logo in company literature, and the

Jaguar was the first standard electric guitar to carry this on its headstock. During the following years Fender gradually applied this new logo to all guitars, and in 1965 began to stamp the modernised 'F' of the logo on to neckplates and later on to their newly-designed machine heads.

The Jaguar had better pickups than the Jazzmaster, looking like Strat units but with metal shielding added at the base and sides, no doubt as a response to the criticisms of the Jazzmaster's tendency to noisiness. The Jag's electrics were even more complex than the Jazzmaster's, using the same rhythm circuit but adding a trio of lead-circuit switches. Like the Jazzmaster, the Jaguar was very popular when introduced. But this top-of-the-range guitar, "one of the finest solid body electric guitars that has ever been offered to the public" in Fender's original sales hyperbole, never enjoyed sustained success.

In 1964 Fender introduced a new model at the lower end of its price-range, the **Mustang**, effectively a Duo-Sonic with vibrato. At first the Mustang shared the slab body of the Duo-Sonic, but Fender gradually introduced a contoured body to all of its 'student' models of the time: the one-pickup Musicmaster, two-pickup Duo-Sonic and vibrato-equipped Mustang. While the existing Duo-Sonic and Musicmaster had previously been available only with a short 22.5in scale, from 1964 together with the new Mustang they were offered in optional 24in-scale versions.

Fender's Successful Sixties

By this time Fender had become a remarkably successful company. Many buildings had been added to cope with increased manufacturing demands, and by 1964 they employed some 600 people, 500 of whom worked in manufacturing. Forrest White says his guitar production staff were making 1500 instruments a week at the end of 1964, compared to the 40 a week Fender had been making when he'd joined the company ten years earlier. As well as electric guitars, Fender's pricelist in 1964 offered amplifiers, steel guitars, electric basses, acoustic guitars, electric pianos, effects units and a host of related accessories. Don Randall remembers writing a million dollars' worth of sales during his first year in the 1950s, which rose to some 10 million dollars' worth in the mid-1960s. By that time the beat boom, triggered by the Beatles and the so-called British Invasion of pop groups, was taking the United States by storm. Electric guitars were at their peak of popularity, and Fender were amongst the biggest and most successful producers.

Exporting had also become important to Fender's huge success, and had started back in 1959 when Randall first visited a European trade show at Frankfurt, Germany. "Our products were known over there because of the GIs playing our guitars," he remembers, "and they were very much prized. So we started doing business over there." Britain was an especially important market in the 1960s because of the worldwide success of its pop groups.

"We were the biggest musical instrument exporter in the United States," remembers Randall, "in fact I think we exported more American-manufactured musical products than all the other companies combined. We had it all to ourselves for maybe three or four years." Western Europe was the biggest export market, but Fender were also doing well in Scandinavia, South Africa, Rhodesia (now Zimbabwe), Japan, Australia, Canada and many others.

$13 Million Worth of Fender

All in all, Fender were extremely successful. Then, in January 1965, the Fender companies were sold to the mighty Columbia Broadcasting System Inc, better known as CBS. A musical instrument trade magazine reported in somewhat shocked tones: "The purchase price of $13 million is by far the highest ever offered in the history of the music [ie musical instrument] industry for any single manufacturer, and was about two million dollars more than CBS paid recently for the New York Yankees baseball team. The acquisition, a sterling proof of the music industry's growth potential, marks the first time

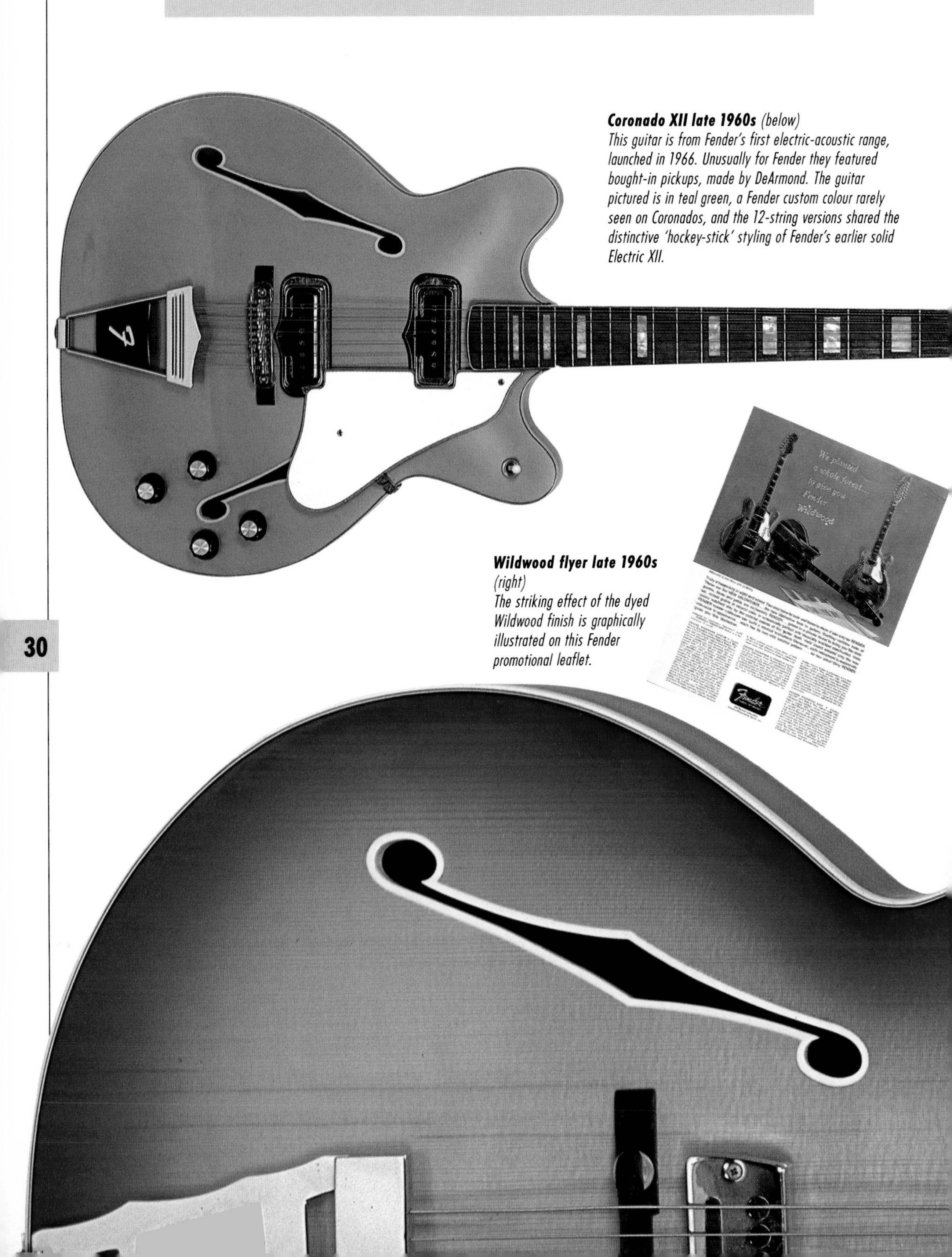

Coronado XII late 1960s *(below)*
This guitar is from Fender's first electric-acoustic range, launched in 1966. Unusually for Fender they featured bought-in pickups, made by DeArmond. The guitar pictured is in teal green, a Fender custom colour rarely seen on Coronados, and the 12-string versions shared the distinctive 'hockey-stick' styling of Fender's earlier solid Electric XII.

Wildwood flyer late 1960s
(right)
The striking effect of the dyed Wildwood finish is graphically illustrated on this Fender promotional leaflet.

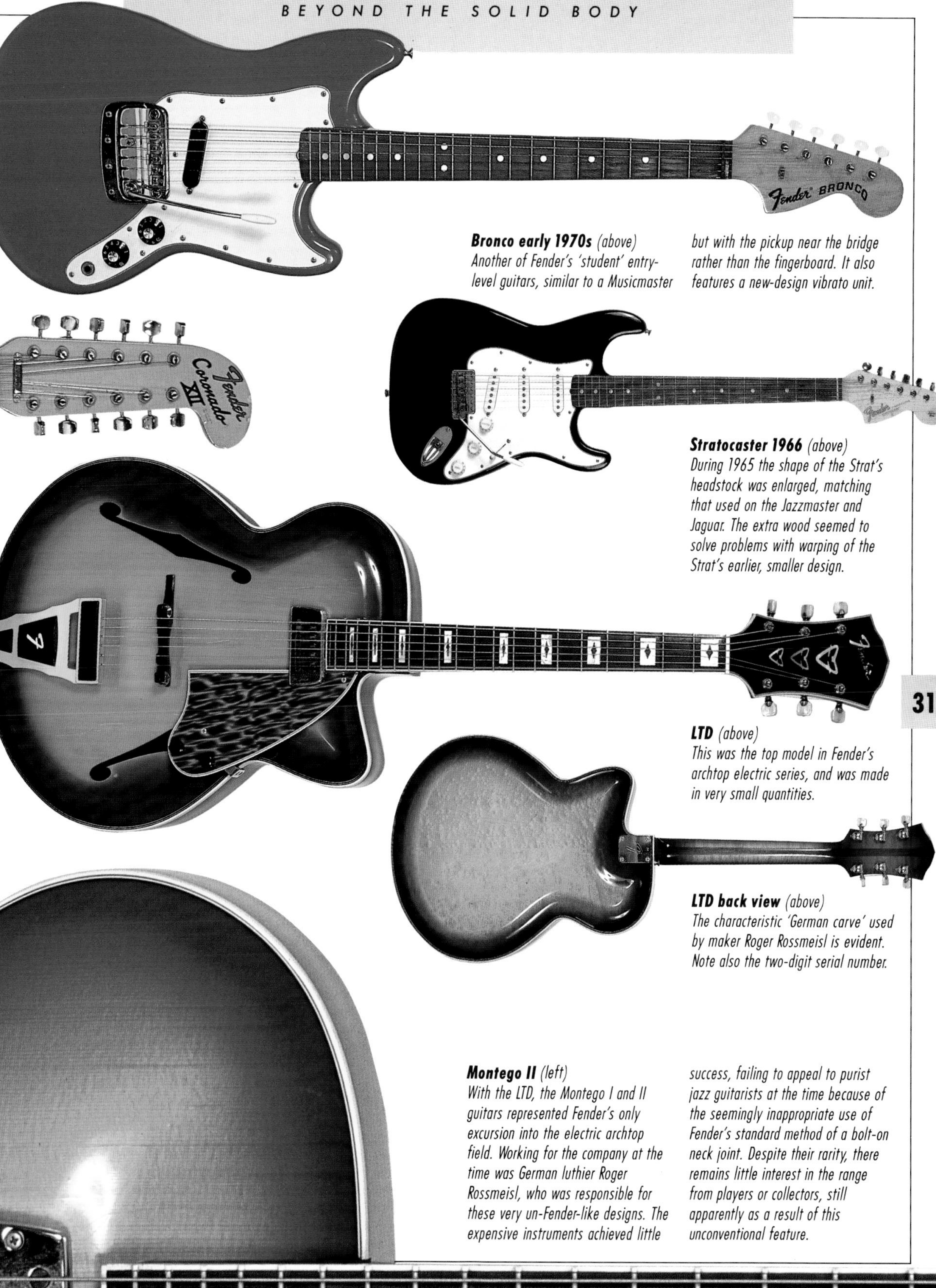

Bronco early 1970s *(above)*
Another of Fender's 'student' entry-level guitars, similar to a Musicmaster but with the pickup near the bridge rather than the fingerboard. It also features a new-design vibrato unit.

Stratocaster 1966 *(above)*
During 1965 the shape of the Strat's headstock was enlarged, matching that used on the Jazzmaster and Jaguar. The extra wood seemed to solve problems with warping of the Strat's earlier, smaller design.

LTD *(above)*
This was the top model in Fender's archtop electric series, and was made in very small quantities.

LTD back view *(above)*
The characteristic 'German carve' used by maker Roger Rossmeisl is evident. Note also the two-digit serial number.

Montego II *(left)*
With the LTD, the Montego I and II guitars represented Fender's only excursion into the electric archtop field. Working for the company at the time was German luthier Roger Rossmeisl, who was responsible for these very un-Fender-like designs. The expensive instruments achieved little success, failing to appeal to purist jazz guitarists at the time because of the seemingly inappropriate use of Fender's standard method of a bolt-on neck joint. Despite their rarity, there remains little interest in the range from players or collectors, still apparently as a result of this unconventional feature.

that one of the nation's largest corporations has entered our field. With sales volume in excess of half a billion dollars annually, CBS currently does more business than the entire music industry does at retail. Actual purchase of Fender was made by the Columbia Records Distribution Division of CBS whose outstanding recent feats have included the production of 'My Fair Lady'."

Economic analysts were advising the big corporations of the time to diversify and acquire companies from a range of different businesses – hence the New York Yankees and, in turn, Fender for CBS. They were doubtless told that all they had to do was finance and expand the new acquisitions, and rich pickings would follow.

Leo Fender was by all accounts a hypochondriac, and the sale was prompted by his acute health worries, principally over the sinus complaint he'd had since the mid-1950s. He told International Musician in 1978: "I thought I was going to have to retire. I had been suffering for years with a virus infection of the sinuses and it made my life a misery. I felt that I wasn't going to be in the health to carry on."

The sale of Fender to CBS was handled by Don Randall, who says that at first Leo had offered him the company for a million-and-a-half dollars. Randall didn't feel he was ready for that kind of career move, so suggested later to Leo that he might see what he could get from an outside buyer. Leo agreed, and Randall's first tentative discussions took place with the Baldwin Piano & Organ Co of Ohio, probably in early 1964. Randall also contacted an investment banker, who at first suggested that Fender go public, which neither Leo nor Randall wished to pursue. The bankers then came up with CBS as a potential purchaser.

"Now we had two companies up there," Randall remembers, "but Baldwin's attitude to purchasing turned out to be totally unsatisfactory for our purposes. So finally we got down to the nitty gritty with Columbia, and I made about half a dozen trips back and forth to New York, jam sessions with attorneys and financial people.

"The guys at CBS came in with a really low price at first, but eventually we came to a fairly agreeable price, and I called Leo and said how does that suit you? He said oh Don, I can't believe it, are you trying to pull my leg? And I said no – does that sound like a satisfactory deal we can close on? 'Well anything you say Don, that's fine, you just go ahead and do it,' he said. And so the rest is history, we went on and sold it to CBS after a lot of investigation, they did a big study on us, people came in to justify the sale and the price paid, and we consummated the deal. Leo wouldn't even go back to New York for the signing, for the pay-off or anything. 'You get the money and you bring it out to me,' he said."

The Pre-CBS Debate

The sale of Fender to CBS has provoked much retrospective consternation among guitar players and collectors, some of whom consider so-called 'pre-CBS' instruments – in other words those made prior to the beginning of 1965 – as superior to those made after that date. This is a rather meaningless generalisation, and it is a pity that such an assumption has become so entrenched. Clearly, it is ludicrous to suggest that a guitar made at the Fender factory on Thursday 31st December 1964 would have a natural superiority over one made the very next day in the same building by the same workers using the same materials and tools. But there can be little doubt that over a period of time after the sale CBS did introduce changes to the production methods of Fender guitars, a proportion of which were detrimental to the quality of some instruments.

According to some insiders, the problem with CBS at this time was that they seemed to believe that it was enough simply to pour lots of money into Fender. And certainly Fender's sales did increase and profits did go up – Randall remembers income almost doubling in the first year that CBS owned Fender. Profit became the number one consideration, says Forrest White, who remained as manager of electric guitar and amplifier production. "Buddy, if you didn't show that profit down there so they could have a good report with the stockholders, well look out! That's the only thing they were concerned about."

Dale Hyatt stayed on as a salesman with CBS. He says: "They put an awful lot of money into that company, enough for it to be the biggest success in the world. They gave them everything they needed to do the job, but they put in the wrong people. They took out the existing people because they didn't have enough education, people who had put it where it was, and shipped in their own people with educational background and degrees. They hired a number of people from a glassware company whom we always referred to as 'cup-and-saucer salesmen', they didn't know a headstock from a tailpiece. Their idea was, and I was told this by one of them, a guitar is no different from a loaf of bread: you put it in a package, and ship it. That's all there is to it."

Forrest White recalls: "CBS had a vice president for everything. I think they had a vice president for cleaning the toilets. You name it, whatever it was, it had a vice president." And Don Randall: "Everybody at CBS was climbing the corporate ladder, stepping on everyone else's fingers as they climbed up. There was a tremendous amount of in-fighting." And George Fullerton: "'When the company was sold, there were four people in the research and development lab. Within a year after CBS got in on it, the R&D [research & development] section was moved away from the factory into another building, and I once counted 65 hourly-paid people on the time-clock over there."

Forrest White recalls a specific example of the cavalier attitude of some of the new staff. "They brought some guy into purchasing, didn't know one thing about musical instruments, but he made this boast that we were paying too much for everything and he was gonna save the company all kinds of money. Someone comes in selling a bunch of magnet wire they wanted to clear out. To this CBS guy, magnet wire was magnet wire, the heck with gauge and coating. So he buys all this crap. And when I found out, I told him we couldn't make our pickups with this stuff, it's not the right specification. But I was told we were going to use it. Now if you can imagine what's happening to the sound of the guitar . . ."

Sloppy Finishes and Three-Bolt Necks

Further opinion on the effect of the CBS takeover on Fender's guitars seems divided among the personnel we spoke to. George Fullerton says that criticisms started coming back from the dealers. "They'd say the guitars don't play like they used to, they aren't adjusted like they used to be." Dale Hyatt reckons that the quality stayed relatively stable until around 1968. And then quality control declined, he says, "and it got to the point where I did not enjoy going to any store anywhere, because every time I walked in I found myself defending some poor piece of workmanship. They got very sloppy with the finish, with far too many bad spots, and the neck sockets were being cut way over size. They blamed that on the new three-bolt neck but it wasn't that – put six bolts in it and it still would have moved. And they created their own competition, let the door wide open for everybody else, including the Japanese."

Randall, who became vice president and general manager of Fender Musical Instruments and Fender Sales under the new owners, thinks the supposition that quality deteriorated when CBS took over is a fallacy. "I will say this for CBS, they were just as interested in quality as we were. They spared no amount of time or effort to ensure the quality was there. There's always this suspicion when a big company takes over that they're going to make a lousy product and sell it for a higher price, and that's not true here. But the other problems that existed were multiple."

Randall points to several examples, including the division of all activities into cost-centres "down to the last nut, bolt and screw" to aid CBS's corporate book-keeping, and the re-writing of the workers' job descriptions. "Everyone went back to work and they were saying, don't tell me to do that, that's not my job! Before,

Swinger 1969 *(left)*
This addition to the Fender range was produced only in 1969. The odd body and headstock shape were achieved by cutting down leftover parts from a variety of existing models, while the hardware was originally intended for the Musicmaster. A small quantity was made, so the Swinger is quite rare, but nonetheless it is simply another 'student'-style Fender with short-scale neck.

Custom 1969/Maverick 1969 *(above)*
Initially, leftover Electric XII necks were used for these models. Fender adapted each headstock for six-string use by removing a section to shorten its length, thus accomodating six machine heads only. The join and original holes were masked by applying a wood veneer to front and back. The side view (above left) shows these modifications. Some examples of this model bear the name Maverick (above right) rather than Custom. Later, Fender manufactured purpose-built necks for the Custom, and naturally these do not have such alterations.

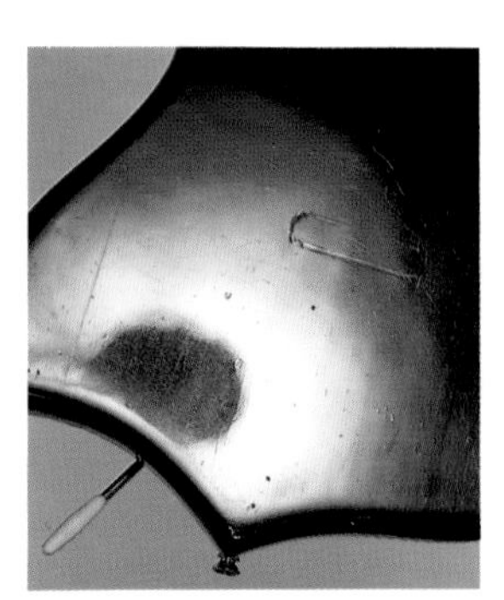

Custom 1970 *(right)*
Another shortlived addition to the Fender range, part of the drive by CBS in the late 1960s to create new models with minimal outlay. Body, neck, pickups and controls were derived from the discontinued Electric XII, while the Mustang provided a suitable vibrato. The Custom was certainly more up-market than the Swinger (above) but the unusual styling did not prove popular and production was therefore limited.

Custom 1970 back view *(above)*
While the Custom's front was normally finished in sunburst, the back was black to hide the modifications necessary to convert the old Electric XII body. Cracks often reveal the crude wooden insert (above) in the back.

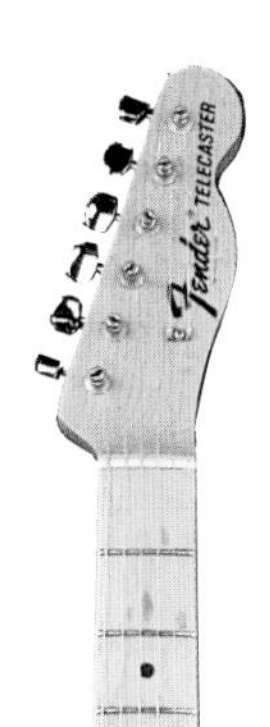

'Paisley' Telecaster late 1960s *(left)*

Fender's interpretation of 1960s Flower Power came in the garish patterns of the 'Paisley Red' and 'Blue Flower' Telecasters. A clear plastic scratchplate revealed the full glory of the designs, achieved by attaching self-adhesive wallpaper to the front and back of the body. The finishes do not wear well, but these Teles are now much sought after.

Thinline Telecaster late 1960s *(right)*

Introduced in 1968, this was intended to reduce the weight of the solid Telecaster by hollowing out sections of the body, and even included a token f-hole as a visual clue to its semi-solid status. It retained standard Tele layout, but with a restyled scratchplate.

'Rosewood' Telecaster late 1960s *(right)*

This exotic Telecaster uses rosewood throughout, a wood more often used for fingerboards. To complement the rich colouring, it was the first Tele to use a black laminated scratchplate. The wood makes for a striking yet heavy guitar, and Fender attempted to lighten the load on later versions by moving to a two-piece body with internal hollowed chambers.

Thinline Telecaster early 1970s *(above)*

In 1971 the Thinline Tele was redesigned to incorporate Fender's new humbucking pickups.

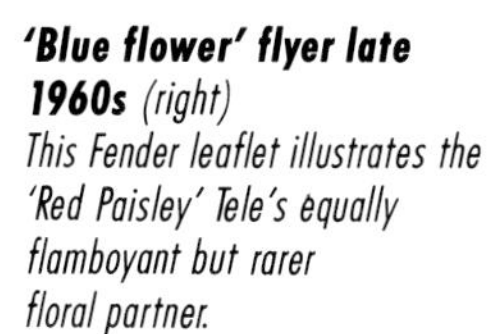

'Blue flower' flyer late 1960s *(right)*

This Fender leaflet illustrates the 'Red Paisley' Tele's equally flamboyant but rarer floral partner.

everyone worked as a team, pushed the product through. Anything that went wrong *now*, it was well, that's not my job, you take care of it. This led to a lot of problems."

Leo, whose services were retained as 'special consultant in research and development', told Guitar Player in 1978 that he didn't think the changes made by CBS had lowered Fender quality. "They weren't trying to cheapen the instrument. Maybe they tried to accelerate production but it was natural for them to do that because on one instrument alone, I think it was the Mustang, we were back-ordered something like 150,000 units. On a back-order of that size, and there were others too, you can't just sit around."

A couple of years after the sale to CBS, Leo changed doctors and was given a huge dose of antibiotics which cured his complaint. He completed a few projects for CBS but left when his five-year contract expired in 1970. He went on to make instruments for the Music Man company and his later G&L operation.

But Leo was not the first of the old guard to leave CBS. Forrest White departed in 1967 "because I wouldn't build some products – the solid state amps – that I thought were unworthy of Leo's name", and went on to work with Leo at Music Man, as well as for CMI (who owned Gibson) and Rickenbacker. Don Randall went in 1969, disenchanted with corporate life, and formed Randall Electric Instruments, which he sold in 1987. George Fullerton left CBS in 1970, worked with Ernie Ball for a while, and with Leo formed the G&L company ('George & Leo') in 1980, though Fullerton left in 1986. Dale Hyatt, who resigned from CBS in 1972, was also part of the G&L set-up, which was sold after Leo Fender's death in March 1991.

TWELVE ELECTRIC STRINGS

Meanwhile at Fender Musical Instruments the **Electric XII**, a guitar that had been on the drawing board when the CBS sale took place, finally hit the music stores in the summer of 1965. Electric 12-strings had recently been popularised by the Beatles and the Byrds, who used Rickenbackers on-stage, so Fender joined in the battle with their own version. There were no surprises in the guitar's body – it was that familiar offset-waist design again (and at $349 the 12-string was pitched at the same price as the Jazzmaster). The Electric XII had a long headstock, necessary to carry the extra machine heads, which finished in a curved end. This distinctive headstock has earned the nickname 'hockey-stick'.

An innovation was the Electric XII's 12-saddle bridge which allowed for precise adjustments of individual string heights and intonation, a luxury hitherto unknown on any 12-string guitar. But the 12-string craze of the 1960s proved shortlived and the Electric XII suffered a similar fate, being dropped from the range in 1968.

THE FENDER THAT NEVER WAS

Uniquely for Fender, a guitar appeared in their 1965/66 literature that never actually made it into production. Naturally a company makes many designs and prototypes which do not translate to commercial release, but for an instrument to get as far as printed sales material and then be withdrawn implies a serious error of judgement somewhere along the line. The guitar was the **Marauder**, and its obvious distinction was summed up by Fender as follows in their hapless catalogue entry: "It appears as though there are no pickups. There are, in reality, however, four newly created pickups mounted *underneath* the pickguard."

The design had been offered to Fender by an individual named Freeman, who apparently had a patent covering his idea of sinking powerful pickups under the scratchplate. Forrest White remembers that there were nonetheless problems with weak signals from the pickups, and George Fullerton says he thinks there was a dispute between Freeman and CBS concerning the patent. Either way, the Marauder never went on sale.

Gene Fields had worked in the factory at Fender since 1961, and was taken on in R&D after the CBS sale. He worked on a second proposed version of the Marauder, probably in 1966, and explained to Guitar Player in 1991 that eight prototypes were built, this time with three conventional pickups plus complex associated control switching. Four prototypes bore slanted frets. "We never got any real excitement when we field-tested it," he recalled. Thus the solitary Marauders finally died.

CBS completed the construction of a new Fender factory in 1966 at a cost of $1.3 million, situated next to Fender's nine buildings on the South Raymond site. Meanwhile some cosmetic changes were being made to various Fender models: in 1965 the Stratocaster gained a broader headstock shape; also that year the fingerboards of the Electric XII, Jaguar and Jazzmaster were bound; and in 1966 the same trio was given block-shaped fingerboard inlays rather than the previous dot markers. Generally, CBS seemed to be fiddling for fiddling's sake.

A firm innovation did, however, come from the new regime, in the shape of a range of hollow-bodied electrics. These were the first electric-acoustics from Fender who until this point were clearly identified in the player's mind as a maker of solid-bodied electrics. Evidently the success of Gibson's ES range of electric-acoustics and to a lesser extent models by Gretsch and others must have tempted CBS and their search for wider markets.

The German Influence

Roger Rossmeisl had been brought into the company by Leo Fender in 1962 to design acoustic guitars, and he also became responsible for the new electric-acoustics. Both acoustics and electric-acoustics were manufactured at Fender's separate acoustic guitar plant on Missile Way in Fullerton.

Rossmeisl, the son of a German guitar-maker, had come to the States in the 1950s and initially worked for Gibson in Michigan, soon moving to Rickenbacker in California where he made a number of one-off custom guitars as well as designing production models such as the Capri and Combo ranges. Rossmeisl also influenced other makers, notably Mosrite of California.

Launched in 1966 the **Coronado** thinline guitars were the first of Rossmeisl's electric designs to appear and, despite their conventional, equal-cutaway, bound bodies with large, stylised f-holes, they employed the standard Fender headstock design and bolt-on neck. Options included a new vibrato tailpiece, and there was also a 12-string version that co-opted the Electric XII's 'hockey-stick' headstock.

Virgilio 'Babe' Simoni had worked for Fender since joining the company at the age of 16 in 1953, and had by the mid-1960s become product manager of stringed instruments. In an interview with Guitar Player in 1984, Simoni remembered a particular problem with the Coronados: "We couldn't get the binding material to stick to them. We'd bind them at night and come back in the morning and the thing would be popped loose. So the company that supplied the binding material told us we were using the wrong material . . . We were re-binding them several times, and the veneer is very thin on them." The team then devised a special white-to-brown shaded finish called Antigua which was applied to some Coronados – covering up the burn marks caused by the re-binding.

In 1967 Fender introduced more unusual coloured versions of the Coronado models, called 'Wildwood'. As pop culture became absorbed with the dazzling, drug-influenced art of psychedelia, so Fender predictably announced the Coronado Wildwoods as "truly a happening in sight and sound" with "exciting rainbow hues of greens, blues and golds". They certainly did look different. The Wildwood effect was achieved by injecting trees during growth, producing in the sawn wood a unique coloured pattern which followed the grain.

"They were beautiful guitars," remembers Don Randall, "but they never went any place. Never caught on." Which was true of the feedback-prone Coronados in general. Fender's first foray into thinline electric-acoustics was not a great success, and the various versions were all dropped from the catalogues by 1971. Rossmeisl, assisted by Simoni, also came up with a

Fender ad 1977 *(above)*
A transmuted alligator did little to help sell the Starcaster.

Starcaster late 1970s *(right)*
This second attempt to crack the semi-acoustic market has much more of a Fender feel to the design, using an offset-waist body and a variation on the company's customary headstock style. Despite its quality, it failed to gain wide acceptance.

Stratocaster late 1970s *(above)*
In the late 1970s Fender revived the antigua finish, first used in the mid 1960s on the Coronado range. Back then the finish was used to disguise manufactuing flaws, but this time the effect was used purely for aesthetic reasons. The reactivated two-tone shaded finish with matching scratchplate was featured on various Fender models, and the black plastic parts used in the late 1970s complemented the visual style of these antigua instruments.

Telecaster Deluxe mid 1970s *(above)*
This Telecaster combined Gibson-like electrics with a Stratocaster neck and a Tele body. A limited number also featured a Strat vibrato unit.

Telecaster Custom late 1970s *(below)*
In the 1970s some players replaced their Tele neck pickups with humbuckers... so Fender obligingly issued just such a guitar in 1972.

Fender catalogue cover 1976 *(above)*

Fender ad 1978 *(right)*
An adman's conception of the frenzied Fender R&D lab. Note the Strat with natural finish and non-vibrato bridge, a fashionable combination at the time.

Stratocaster 1973 *(below)*
A new truss-rod system was introduced to some models by Fender in 1971, together with a three-bolt neck fixing. This guitar shows the new 'bullet' truss-rod adjuster at headstock.

lightweight version of the Tele in 1968, the **Thinline Telecaster**, with three hollowed-out cavities inside the body and a modified scratchplate shaped to accommodate the single, token f-hole.

Another reaction to the psychedelic style of the late 1960s came when Fender applied paisley or floral patterned self-adhesive wallpaper to some Telecasters in order to give them flower-power appeal. This was shortlived. In 1967 Fender launched another of their 'student' solid electrics, the $150 **Bronco** with single pickup and simple vibrato.

ARCHTOP FENDERS

The following year Roger Rossmeisl was let loose with a couple of guitar designs that were even less like the normal run of Fenders than the Coronado models. Roger's speciality was the so-called 'German carve' taught to him by his father, Wenzel. It gives a distinctive indented 'lip' around the top edge of the body, following its outline. Rossmeisl adopted this feature for the new hollow-body archtop electric **Montego** and **LTD** models, all eminently traditional but still obstinately using Fender's customary bolt-on neck. From all reports there were very few of these made, and there is some evidence to suggest that a number may even have been recalled.

Rossmeisl did not last much longer at Fender. "He had a drinking problem," says White, "and finally we had to let him go because of it." George Fullerton echoes a general feeling when he says, "Roger was a marvellous designer and didn't become the person he should have been. I think he was his own worst enemy. Such a waste." Rossmeisl died in Germany in 1979 at the age of 52.

Toward the end of the 1960s came firm evidence of CBS wringing every last drop of potential income from unused factory stock that would otherwise have been written off. Two shortlived guitars, the **Custom** and the **Swinger**, were assembled from these leftovers, as Babe Simoni recalled in Guitar Player in 1984. "Production was way down, and we had a bunch of Electric XII necks and bodies. They asked if anyone had any ideas on what to do with them before they scrapped them out. That's when I converted them to six-strings and carved the bodies into a different design." This was the Custom, although originally, according to Simoni, it was called the Maverick. "First we made those from scrap material, then someone in engineering got the bright idea to make hard tooling for it, and they did tool up and actually produced Customs."

Dale Hyatt remembers the headache which the Maverick/Custom concoction caused the salesmen. "It was an abortion. Everybody knows what it was: a way to get rid of stuff. But people out there in the field are smarter than that. The dealers are smarter, they know. The musicians know better. But CBS didn't care, they made 'em and said here, you go sell 'em."

The Swinger was made from unused Musicmaster or Bass V bodies mated with unpopular short-scale Mustang necks. Simoni again: "Instead of using the Mustang headstock design which was something like a Strat's I made it more rounded like an acoustic's. Then somebody came along and cut the end of it off – made it look like a spear. And the body was chopped up and changed a little bit . . . We never tooled up for them like we did with the Custom." Both the Maverick/Custom and the Swinger were made in necessarily limited numbers. The Swinger never appeared officially in Fender's literature, while the Custom made the 1970 catalogue and was on that year's pricelists at $299.50.

Toward the end of the 1960s Strats took a boost when a wild, inspired guitarist by the name of Jimi Hendrix applied the Fender's sensuous curves to his live cavorting and studio experimentation. Salesman Dale Hyatt recalls: "When guys like that came along, we couldn't build enough of them. As a matter of fact I think Jimi Hendrix caused more Stratocasters to be sold than all the Fender salesmen put together!"

One of the few top bands conspicuously absent from Fender usage was The Beatles, although this had not been through lack of trying on Don Randall's part. Earlier in the 1960s he'd tried to persuade Beatles' manager Brian Epstein to get his boys into Fender. "It was the only time we ever tried to buy somebody off," Randall says. "I sent a member of my staff to try and buy Brian Epstein off. But no, it was a pittance . . . "

Later, probably in 1969, Randall managed to secure a meeting with Lennon and McCartney at the band's Apple headquarters in London. "I was still kind of interested in getting them to use our products. So we went up there and had quite a long conversation with Paul, he had some great ideas, real animated guy. Finally John and Yoko came in, and we all sat down at this big conference table." The results were the band's Fender-Rhodes pianos and George Harrison's **Rosewood Telecaster**, all used in the 'Let It Be' movie.

The 1970s are believed by many players and collectors to be the poorest years of Fender's production history, and there can be little doubt that quality control slipped and more low-standard Fenders were made during this decade than any other. But some fine Fender guitars were made in the 1970s as well. It's just that there were more average guitars made than good guitars, and it often seems as if the good ones were produced in spite of rather than because of the company's activities.

During the 1970s the CBS management cut back on the existing Fender product lines and produced hardly any new models. The last Esquires were made in 1970, the year in which the Duo-Sonic died. The Jaguar disappeared in about 1975, and in 1980 the Bronco, Jazzmaster, Musicmaster and Thinline Tele had all been phased out of production, by which time Fender were pretty much dependent on their ever-reliable Strats and Teles. The newly-important calculations of the balance sheet appeared to be taking precedence over the company's former creativity.

There were a handful of new items, but even these were mostly variations on familiar themes. Part of Fender's distinction had come from their use of bright-sounding single-coil pickups; the warmer, fatter-sounding humbucking types were always seen then as a Gibson mainstay. Nonetheless, in keeping with changing market trends, the Telecaster was given a humbucking pickup at the neck position to create the **Telecaster Custom** in 1972, and similar dabbling led to a sort of Tele-meets-Strat-meets-Gibson, the two-humbucker, Strat-necked **Telecaster Deluxe** of 1973. Both had gone by 1981, the same year the Mustang went.

An anniversary edition of the Stratocaster was issued to celebrate the guitar's first 25 years, a silver-finished Strat with an uninspiring 'ANNIVERSARY' logo on the body's upper horn. The earliest examples were in a new white finish which unfortunately cracked spectacularly. Many were recalled and the main production changed to a more appropriate silver finish. "The quantity, naturally, is limited," announced Fender, who proceeded to make thousands of the **25th Anniversary Stratocaster** during 1979 and 1980. "They went fast in '54. They'll go fast now," ran the over-confident blurb.

The company made another attempt at electric-acoustics with the ill-fated **Starcaster** in 1976, again aimed at competing with Gibson's ever-popular ES range. Designer Gene Fields recalled in Guitar Player in 1991: "When I started with the Starcaster it was to use up the old Coronado parts . . . but during the field test reports somebody said it's a great guitar – and we see you've finally found a way to use up your old scrap. So [vice-president] Dave Gupton said forget it, start over and get me a new design . . . Then when Mudge Miller got in as vice president, Teles and Strats were real hot and he closed the Starcaster down because he didn't want the production time wasted on it." The $850 Starcaster left the Fender list within four years.

DEPARTMENTALISM AT CBS

By 1976 Fender had a five-acre facility under one roof in Fullerton and employed over 750 workers. A company document from that year gives an insight into the rigidly planned steps arranged for any proposed guitar. "A – The idea for the new product is presented to our R&D department. B – The first prototype is made by R&D. C – Our field research technician takes the guitar out for

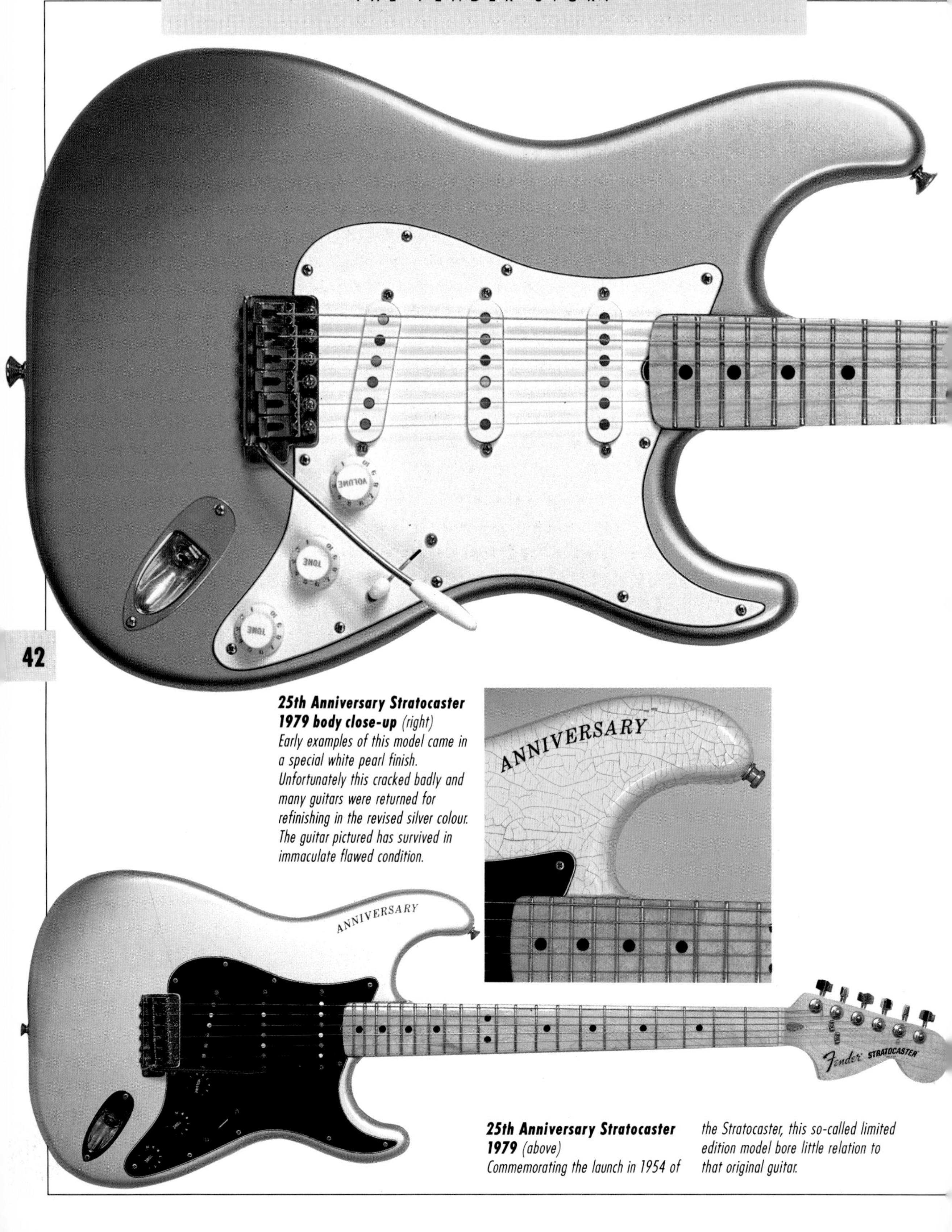

25th Anniversary Stratocaster 1979 body close-up *(right)*
Early examples of this model came in a special white pearl finish. Unfortunately this cracked badly and many guitars were returned for refinishing in the revised silver colour. The guitar pictured has survived in immaculate flawed condition.

25th Anniversary Stratocaster 1979 *(above)*
Commemorating the launch in 1954 of the Stratocaster, this so-called limited edition model bore little relation to that original guitar.

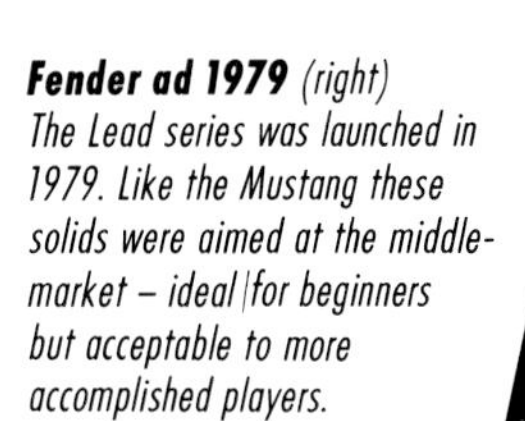

Fender ad 1979 *(right)*
The Lead series was launched in 1979. Like the Mustang these solids were aimed at the middle-market – ideal for beginners but acceptable to more accomplished players.

'Gold' Stratocaster 1981 *(below)*
This Stratocaster featured a gold-painted body and gold-plated hardware. It was one model in Fender's Collector's Series of the early 1980s, as indicated by its C-prefix serial number. This limited edition model used a neck as fitted to the Strat (see below) which, unusually for the time, reverted to a four-bolt fixing and old-style truss-rod adjustment at the body end.

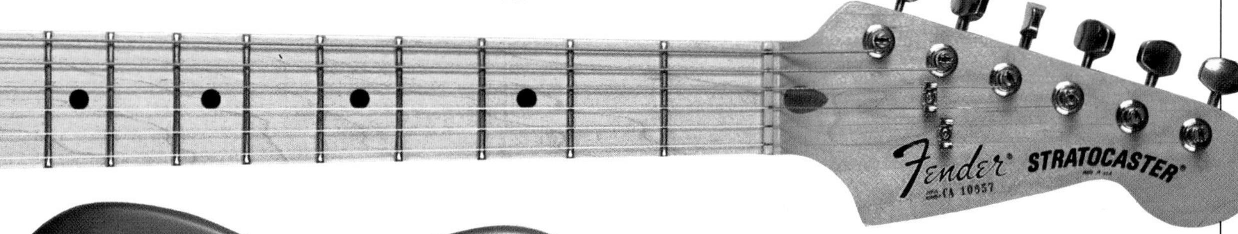

Strat 1980 *(below)*
This model, launched in 1980 and officially using the common abbreviation, reflected trends at the time for brass hardware and 'hot' bridge pickups.

Fender catalogue 1981 *(left)*
This page shows the range of finishes available at the time (including international colours): arctic white; morocco red; monaco yellow; maui blue; capri orange; sahara taupe; cathay ebony; sienna sunburst; and cherry sunburst.

Stratocasters 1981 *(right)*
During the 1970s the range of colours for Stratocasters had dwindled, but in 1980 an expanded, lurid selection appeared briefly, collectively known as international colours. The trio shown use a transitional combination of white laminated scratchplates and black pickup covers and knobs.

field testing. A cross section of the local vicinity is used and a variety of groups and individuals are involved. D – After several weeks of field tests, the unit is brought back to R&D and modifications are made if necessary. E – When the product has completed its field tests the final OK is given by the marketing department. Prices are determined and sales forecasts presented to Management and Manufacturing. F – The prototype plus drawings and specifications are then turned over to Manufacturing. G – Manufacturing will then order all necessary parts and machinery to produce the product. H – Engineers prepare assembly aids to inform the various departments of the step-by-step procedures used to get the product to the Finish Department and the ultimate consumer."

John Page, who went on to run Fender's Custom Shop from the late 1980s, started working for Fender in 1978, spending some months on the production line before moving to R&D. He comments on the departmentalism of Fender in the late 1970s. "You couldn't even tell Purchasing what part you wanted or where you wanted it from, all you could tell them was the spec of the part you wanted. It was so compartmentalised, and virtually no-one knew anyone else in another department. There was no communication."

Page also recalls his horror when he discovered one of the CBS executives at the time cheerfully disposing of Fender's history. "He came through our office and he was putting green dots on all our guitars. I asked what he was doing. 'Oh well, I got this great programme, I'm gonna give these away to dealers, yes sir.' What! And before we were able to stop it he had given away about 80 per cent of our original prototypes and samples," Page sighs.

STUDENT LEADS

One of Page's colleagues in R&D at the time was Gregg Wilson, who designed a new 'student' guitar to replace the Musicmaster, Bronco, Duo-Sonic, and Mustang. These were the **Lead** I and II guitars of 1979, simple double-cutaway solids, though not desperately cheap at $399. Page himself designed a later variation, the Lead III, but none of the Leads lasted beyond 1982. Wilson told Guitar Player of a joke heard around Fender at the time: "We don't build them like we used to, and we never did."

Page's next project was a fresh stab at budget-priced solids with the single-cutaway **Bullet** series. The Bullets began production in 1981, but Fender decided for the first time in its history to shift manufacturing outside the United States, to eliminate tooling costs. Joining a general trend in the early 1980s among many guitar companies both Western and Eastern, Fender decided to try Korean manufacture. Page remembers early samples. "In comes this guitar with half-inch action and yeah, it's like that because we got it real cheap. So back they went." Fender decided not to have the Bullets made entirely in Korea, and so at first they were assembled in the States using Korean-manufactured parts. But even this method did not produce guitars of a high enough standard, and by late 1981 the Bullets were back to full American production, and Fender's first experience of oriental manufacturing was over. The Bullets lasted until 1983, and in that year various shortlived double-cutaway versions were produced.

Another Gregg Wilson design from this period was the **Strat** – an official use, at last, of the oft-used affectionate abbreviation. The Strat combined standard Stratocaster visuals with updated circuitry and fashionable heavy-duty brass hardware. The intention was also to re-introduce the old-style narrow headstock of the original Stratocasters, but unfortunately worn-out tooling was used which delivered a not entirely accurate re-creation.

HEADHUNTING THE FUTURE

In the early 1980s the CBS management appear to have decided that they needed some new blood to help reverse the decline in Fender's fortunes. Income had been climbing spectacularly until 1980 – it had tripled in that year from 1971's $20 million – but re-investment in the company was wavering. During 1981 key personnel were recruited from Yamaha's American musical instrument organisation. John McLaren was brought in to head up CBS Musical Instruments overall, and among the other newcomers from Yamaha were Bill Schultz and Dan Smith. Schultz was hired as Fender president and Smith as director of marketing, electric guitars.

Smith recalls: "We were brought in to kind of turn the reputation of Fender around, and to get it so it was making money again. It was starting to lose money, and at that point in time everybody hated Fender. We thought we knew how bad it was. We took it for granted that they could make Stratocasters and Telecasters the way they used to make them, but we were wrong. So many things had been changed in the plant."

Schultz was given the go-ahead by CBS to try to improve matters. One of the first changes Smith made on his arrival was to revise the overall spec of the Stratocaster, reverting to what was generally felt to be the more stable four-bolt neck/body joint (as used from 1954 to 1971 when CBS brought in the three-bolt joint). "We also changed it to the *right* headstock," says Smith, referring to the revamped Strat's adoption of a neater version based on the pre-1965 head shape. "We had a lot of stock to use up, and we couldn't release the four-bolt until the three-bolt was gone." The 'four-bolt' **Standard Strat** started to come off the line at Fender's Fullerton plant toward the end of 1981.

Smith recalls an early shock as he toured the factory, before the 'four-bolts' had come on-stream. "I remember looking at the body contours. People were complaining about contours, and here's a rack of 2000 guitars. Every one of them had a different edge contour! We also went and pulled guitars out of the warehouse and did general re-inspections on them, 800-and-something guitars, and out of those I think only about 15 passed the *existing* criteria. So we sat down and re-wrote the criteria."

The Machine Stops

Schultz recommended a large investment package, primarily aimed at modernising the factory. This had the immediate effect of virtually stopping production while new machinery was brought in and the staff was re-trained. Another recommendation that Schultz had been working on was to start alternative production of Fenders in Japan. The reason was relatively straightforward: Fender's sales were being hammered by the onslaught of orientally-produced copies. These Japanese copyists made their biggest profits in their domestic market, so the best place to hit back at them was in Japan – by making and selling guitars there.

Oriental Emulation

When the Japanese had started emulating classic American guitars in the early 1970s, most Western makers didn't see much to worry about. Later, the quality of the Japanese instruments improved, but some American makers still kept their heads stuck firmly in the sand. As Dave Gupton, vice president of Fender back in 1978, told Guitar Player: "Fender is not adversely affected by the Japanese copies as perhaps some of the other major manufacturers, because we have been able to keep our costs pretty much in line." That casual attitude changed dramatically in a few short years. By the dawn of the 1980s the dollar had soared in value relative to the yen. Coupled with the high quality of many Japanese guitars, this meant that instruments built in the orient were making a real impact on the market – and many of them were copies of the Fender Stratocaster, which was enjoying renewed popularity.

"We had to stop this plethora of copies," says Smith. "A lot of these companies basically told Bill Schultz and I that they were going to bury us. They were ripping us off, and what we really needed to do was to get these guys where it hurt – back in their own marketplace."

So, with the blessing of CBS, negotiations began with two Japanese distributors, Kanda Shokai and Yamano Music, to establish the Fender Japan company, and the joint venture was officially established in March 1982. There are six votes on the Fender Japan board: Fender USA have three, Kanda two and Yamano one. Fender USA also have 38 per cent of the total stock. "More important

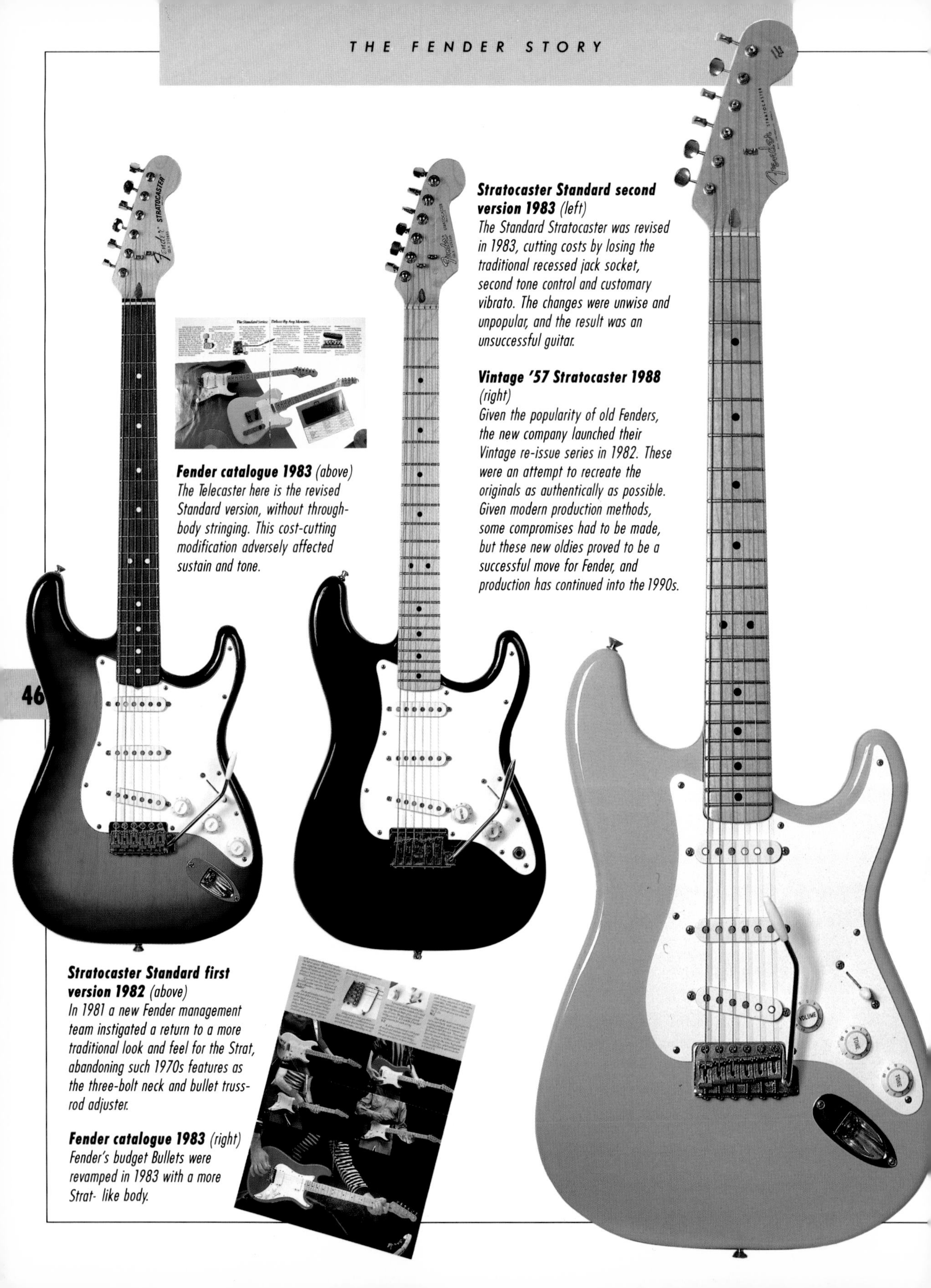

Stratocaster Standard second version 1983 *(left)*
The Standard Stratocaster was revised in 1983, cutting costs by losing the traditional recessed jack socket, second tone control and customary vibrato. The changes were unwise and unpopular, and the result was an unsuccessful guitar.

Vintage '57 Stratocaster 1988 *(right)*
Given the popularity of old Fenders, the new company launched their Vintage re-issue series in 1982. These were an attempt to recreate the originals as authentically as possible. Given modern production methods, some compromises had to be made, but these new oldies proved to be a successful move for Fender, and production has continued into the 1990s.

Fender catalogue 1983 *(above)*
The Telecaster here is the revised Standard version, without through-body stringing. This cost-cutting modification adversely affected sustain and tone.

Stratocaster Standard first version 1982 *(above)*
In 1981 a new Fender management team instigated a return to a more traditional look and feel for the Strat, abandoning such 1970s features as the three-bolt neck and bullet truss-rod adjuster.

Fender catalogue 1983 *(right)*
Fender's budget Bullets were revamped in 1983 with a more Strat- like body.

Elite Telecaster 1983 *(left)*
Fender decided to update the Telecaster with the up-market Elite version, launched in 1983. It featured two new-design humbucking pickups linked to active circuitry, providing a wide array of sounds. The bridge/tailpiece was also restyled, with six individual saddles. On the Gold Elite example shown the optional stick-on scratchplate has been left off.

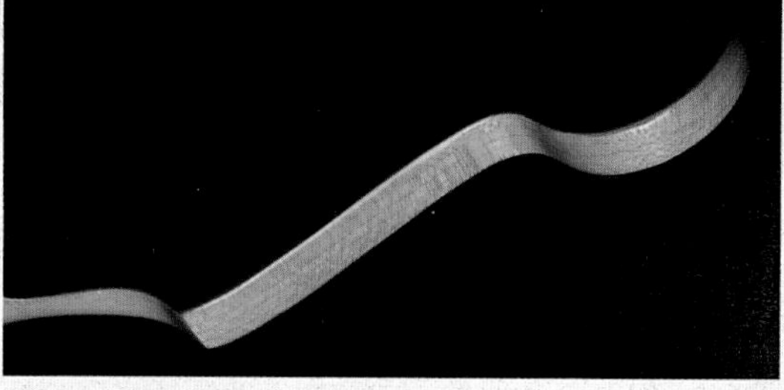

Fender catalogue 1982 *(above)*
The brochure emphasises Fender's long association with top players. Pictured on this cover are Buddy Holly, James Burton, The Ventures, Steve Cropper, Jimi Hendrix and Eric Clapton.

Stratocaster Elite 1983 *(right)*
The Stratocaster received similar treatment to the Elite Tele (above). Three redesigned pickups were fitted, together with a hum-cancelling dummy coil and active circuit. A more obvious change came with the replacement of the five-way selector by three pushbuttons. The new Freeflyte vibrato was an operational disaster, and a major contributor to the model's failure. This example comes in unusual 'stratoburst'

Fender ad 1982 *(above)*
This British advertisement shows a collection of Fender models of the period, including the Black & Gold Telecaster, Strat Walnut, and Vintage Telecaster.

than control of the board, we own the licenses," Smith clarifies. "We license them to build the products, so we really are in control. Of course Fender Japan determine which models they need for their own market, although we have final approval."

After discussions with Tokai, Kawai and others, the factory finally chosen to build guitars for Fender Japan was Fuji Gen-Gakki, based in Matsumoto, some 130 miles north-west of Tokyo. Fuji was best known in the west for the excellence of their Ibanez-branded instruments. "Kanda Shokai had been selling Greco copies of Fender," recalls Smith, "and Fuji had been making those, so to be honest they were pretty well prepared to make Fender guitars."

Copying the Copies

In the States the new management team were working on a strategy to return Fender to its former glory. The plan was for Fender in effect to copy themselves, by recreating the guitars that many players and collectors were spending large sums of money to acquire: the 'vintage' Fenders of the 1950s and 1960s. These early guitars had become so highly prized that the various methods used by collectors and dealers to tell the date of manufacture of a Fender had assumed great importance. It's instructive, therefore, to hear Forrest White, who ran the Fender factory during the 'vintage' period, on the accuracy of serial number translations. "I get so sick and tired of these people who can tell you what year the guitars were made by serial number," says White. "That's a bunch of crap: we had no system. In the early years 5000 was a run. So you make the neckplates, all serial-numbered. You dunk them in a pan, take them to the plater. Come back, dunk them in a bin. Now they're all mixed up. Now let's say I had 10 production runs. The one I ran first, it's still at the bottom of the bin. There's no way, rhyme nor reason to it. So when I read that stuff on dating, I call it Fender fiction." Same with the end-of-neck dates, says White: "We had eight-foot long racks for necks, and the worker picking out necks would, of course, take necks from the point closest to them. So they bring in some more necks, OK? And the necks on the end, they just sat there. So when these guys start with their all-knowing crystal balls, would you please tell them that you spoke to the guy who ran the place?"

At Fender in 1985 the new team needed accurate information to assist in their proposed re-creations of vintage instruments, so R&D man John Page travelled with Dan Smith to a vintage guitar dealer in Illinois. There they took as many measurements and photographs and paint-tests as they could from the relevant vintage Fenders. "We left having bought perfect examples of each era, too," says Smith. "We spent $5600 on a '57 Precision, '60 Jazz Bass, and a '61 Strat. Which for Fender at the time was ludicrous. We went out and bought back our own product!"

Such industry resulted in the **Vintage** re-issue series. The guitars consisted of maple-necked '57 and rosewood-fingerboard '62 Strats, and a '52 Telecaster (the latter project having been started by Freddie Tavares in R&D before Smith and Schultz's arrival). The Vintage reproductions were not exact enough for some die-hard Fender collectors, but generally the guitars were praised and welcomed. The vintage years allocated to the Strat re-issues were chosen, as Smith recalls, "because in the USA 1957 is the classic year for automobiles," and, rather more Fender-related, because 1962 was the transition year for a change in fingerboard construction. "We knew that the vintage guys liked the slab board, so we felt that if we had neck problems we could always go to the curved fretboard and still call it a '62 without scrapping our pricelists and catalogues." Smith also notes that 1962 has no bad memories for most Americans.

Production of the Vintage re-issues had begun in 1982 both at Fender USA and at Fender Japan, but the changes being instituted at Fullerton meant that the USA versions did not come fully on-stream until early 1983. "In fact," says Smith, "I don't really think the factory was running the way we needed it to until probably the first of '84." Dan Smith and co received samples of the Japanese-made

Vintage re-issues before USA production started, and he remembers his team's reaction to the quality of these instruments: "Everybody came up to inspect them and the guys almost cried, because the Japanese product was so good – it was what we were having a hell of a time trying to do."

The Start of Squier

Fender Japan's guitars at this stage were made only for the internal Japanese market, but Fender's European agents were putting pressure on the Fullerton management: a budget-priced Fender was needed to compete with the multitude of exported models being sold in Europe and elsewhere by other Japanese manufacturers.

So Fender Japan made some less costly versions of the Vintage re-issues for European distribution. These were distinguished at first by the addition of a small **Squier Series** logo to the tip of the headstock. This was soon changed, with a large 'Squier' brand replacing the Fender logo. Thus the Squier brand was born. The name came from a string-making company, V C Squier of Michigan, that CBS had acquired in 1965.

Toward the end of 1983, with the USA factory still not up to the scale of production the team wanted, Schultz and Smith decided to have Fender Japan build an instrument for the USA market. Smith: "I said in order not to impact the sales of USA-made instruments, we should have them build us a good three-bolt big-headstock bullet-truss-rod Strat. We needed the income." The result was the appearance on the USA market of what is sometimes known as 'the Squier three-bolt' and in Britain as the **Popular** model. This, together with the earlier Squier Strats and Teles, heralded the sale of Fender Japan products around the world.

"The Squier three-bolt really taught us, contrary to what the guys believed at Fender six or seven years before, that people would buy Fender guitars with 'made in Japan' on them," Smith affirms. "In fact I really believe that our introduction of those instruments, worldwide and in the USA, was what legitimised buying Japanese guitars." Certainly there had at one period been a resistance by many musicians to the cheap image associated with Japanese-made guitars, but the rise in quality of the instruments from brands such as Ibanez, Yamaha, Fernandes, Aria, Tokai – and Fender and Squier – wiped away a good deal of this prejudice and gave oriental guitars a new popularity and respectability.

At the USA factory in 1983 some cost-cutting changes were made to the **Standard Strat** and Telecaster. These were the result of the dollar's strength and the consequent difficulty in selling USA-made products overseas, where they were becoming increasingly high-priced. Savings had to be made, so the Strat lost a tone control and its distinctive jack-socket plate, while the Tele was deprived of its tone-enhancing through-body stringing. These were ill-conceived changes, and many onlookers who had applauded the improvements made since '81 groaned inwardly at the familiar signs of economics once again taking precedence over playability and sound. Fortunately, these mutant guitars lasted only until the end of 1984.

Elite Complications

Another shortlived pair from the same time was the **Elite** Stratocaster and Telecaster, intended as radical new up-market versions of the old faithfuls. Unfortunately the vibrato-equipped Elite Strat came saddled with a terrible bridge, which is what most players recall when the Elites are mentioned. In-fighting at Fender had led to last-minute modifications to the vibrato design and the result was an unwieldy, unworkable piece of hardware. The Elite Strat also featured three pushbuttons for pickup selection, which were not to the taste of players brought up on the classic Fender switch. There were good points – the new pickups, the effective active circuitry, and an improved truss-rod design – but they tended to be overlooked. The Elites were also dropped in 1984.

Three newly-designed Fender ranges were introduced in 1984, made by Fender Japan and intended to compete

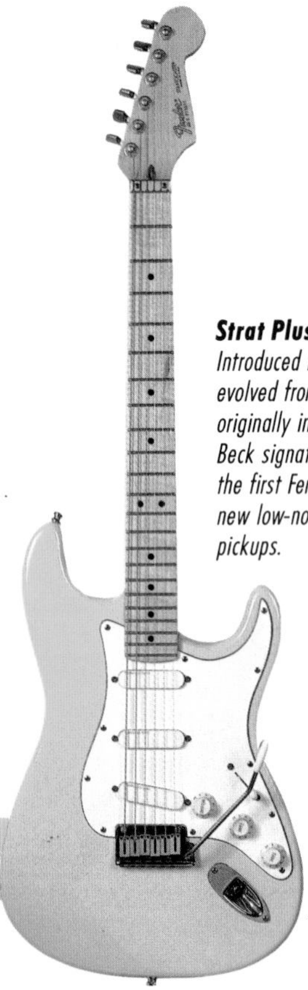

***Strat Plus 1990** (left)*
Introduced in 1987, this guitar evolved from a design originally intended as a Jeff Beck signature guitar. It was the first Fender to carry the new low-noise Lace Sensor pickups.

***Prodigy II 1991** (right)*
A revised body shape graced the new Prodigy of 1991, and the guitar has the fashionable layout of a humbucker at the bridge in addition to the two single-coil units. The II has a locking vibrato unit and locking nut, popularised in the 1980s by high-tech players needing tuning stability. The Prodigy and Prodigy II were among the first guitars to be worked on at Fender's new factory in Ensenada, Mexico (established 1990) although final assembly took place in the US facility.

Thank You.
Fender

***Fender ad 1991** (above)*
When Leo Fender died in March 1991 aged 82 the guitar world mourned the loss of one of its best-known figures. Despite Leo having had no direct link with the company for over 20 years, Fender placed this simple and moving tribute in the music press later that year.

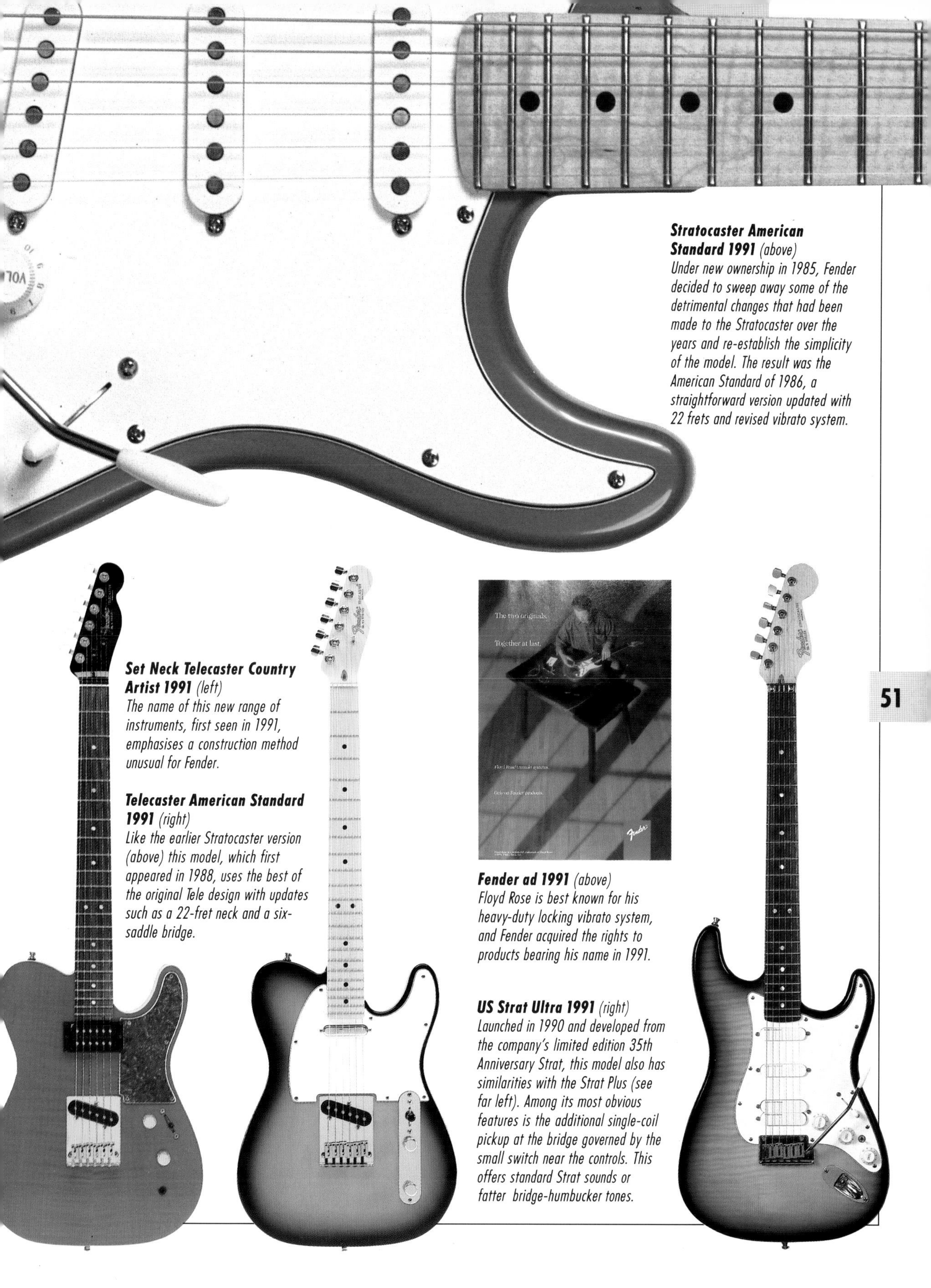

Stratocaster American Standard 1991 *(above)*
Under new ownership in 1985, Fender decided to sweep away some of the detrimental changes that had been made to the Stratocaster over the years and re-establish the simplicity of the model. The result was the American Standard of 1986, a straightforward version updated with 22 frets and revised vibrato system.

Set Neck Telecaster Country Artist 1991 *(left)*
The name of this new range of instruments, first seen in 1991, emphasises a construction method unusual for Fender.

Telecaster American Standard 1991 *(right)*
Like the earlier Stratocaster version (above) this model, which first appeared in 1988, uses the best of the original Tele design with updates such as a 22-fret neck and a six-saddle bridge.

Fender ad 1991 *(above)*
Floyd Rose is best known for his heavy-duty locking vibrato system, and Fender acquired the rights to products bearing his name in 1991.

US Strat Ultra 1991 *(right)*
Launched in 1990 and developed from the company's limited edition 35th Anniversary Strat, this model also has similarities with the Strat Plus (see far left). Among its most obvious features is the additional single-coil pickup at the bridge governed by the small switch near the controls. This offers standard Strat sounds or fatter bridge-humbucker tones.

with some of Gibson's electric guitars. The overall name for the new instruments was the **Master Series**, encompassing electric archtop **D'Aquisto** models and semi-solid **Esprit** and **Flame** guitars. Significantly, they were the first Fender Japan products to be sold outside Japan which had the Fender rather than Squier headstock logo, and the first Fenders with glued-in necks. Their overtly Gibson image was to be their undoing, as Dan Smith admits: "They were made real well, they sounded good and everything else . . . but they weren't 'Fender'. Also, Fuji had manufacturing problems and we didn't get any for over a year. So we introduced them to all this excitement, and nothing came out for a year. And then CBS pulled the plug."

The End for CBS

For a variety of reasons, CBS decided during 1984 that they had finally had enough of this part of the music business, and that they wished to sell Fender Musical Instruments. Smith has his own theory about the way he and Schultz were brought into Fender in 1981 and the circumstances leading up to the sale decision: "I believe that CBS had planned on selling the company all along – and that's just my supposition, I don't have any proof for that. But I think that was probably in the works. They were hoping that we would straighten it out and get it to the point where it was saleable. I like to tell people we had four-and-a-half years where we delivered loaves and fishes, and they wanted us to walk on water. We just didn't do the right miracle."

CBS invited offers for Fender and among the interested parties were the International Music Co (IMC) who marketed Hondo and Jackson guitars among others, and the Kaman Music Corp, best known for Ovation guitars. "Mid to late November of 1984, CBS finally said look, we're not going to have any success selling this for what we want," recalls Smith. "We're getting all these low-ball offers, we'd like to offer it to you guys. If you can raise the capital we'll sell you the company, as long as your offer is better than liquidation. To be honest, if nobody had come up with an offer better than liquidation, Fender would have gone under. That would have been it. Over. Done."

But at the end of January 1985, almost exactly 20 years since they had acquired it, CBS confirmed they would sell Fender to "an investor group led by William Schultz, president of Fender Musical Instruments". The contract was formalised in February and the sale completed in March for $12.5 million. It is interesting to compare this with the price CBS originally paid for the company back in 1965.

With the hectic months of negotiations and financing behind them, Schultz and his team could now run Fender for themselves (and a number of investment banks, of course). The problems they faced were legion, but probably the most immediate was the fact that the Fullerton buildings were not included in the deal (CBS sold the factories separately). So USA production of Fenders stopped in February 1985, although the new team had been stockpiling bodies and necks, and had acquired some existing inventory of completed guitars as well as production machinery. The company went from employing over 800 people in early 1984 down to just over 100 in early 1985. Scary but exciting is how Smith described it at the time: "We're not going to be in the position to make any mistakes. There'll be nobody behind us with a big cheque-book if we have a bad month."

Administration headquarters were established in Brea, not far from Fullerton (and six years later Fender moved admin from Brea to Scottsdale, Arizona). A new factory also had to be found, but in the meantime Schultz and Smith considered using existing production sources further afield – including Godin in Canada. These options proved unworkable, and Fender began searching for a factory site in the general Orange County area of Los Angeles.

Fender had been working on a couple of radical guitar designs before the sale campaign started, and these instruments became victims of the crossfire. One was a

John Page design, the **Performer**, which started life intended for USA production. But with nowhere to build it in the States, Fender shifted it to the Fuji factory in Japan.

The Performer had a distinctive body shape, twin slanted pickups, 24 frets, and an arrow-shaped headstock quite different from the usual Fender Strat derivative. The headstock was in fact based on the 1969 Swinger head, to avoid the need for a new trademark, and was a reaction to the newly popular so-called 'superstrat' design popularised by American guitar-maker Jackson. Among other appointments the superstrat boasted a much-emulated drooping, pointed headstock. All in, the Performer was a thoroughly modern Fender, with few nods to the company's illustrious past.

"We had players lining up to play the Performer," remembers Smith, "but they wanted an American-made product. We had a great response at the New Orleans trade show, but right after that was when CBS pulled the plug. I think it was a great guitar, but it just got caught up in the midst of the sale. The same thing happened with the Master series – we just started to get some players, we just started to do some advertising, and the word came down that it was over, and we basically had to kill all those projects." The Performer did manage to stay on Fender's books until 1986, but it seemed a pity that such a relatively brave move should have been dropped for reasons largely unconnected with the instrument itself.

Of less interest was the **Katana**, a response to another fashion of the time among guitar makers, the weird body shape. Key dealers pressured Bill Schultz to produce an odd-shaped Fender. "I said look, these things are revolting, ugly," recalls Smith. "If somebody plays it, that's what makes it famous. But to pacify the dealers we needed something. So I sat down with the art program on the Macintosh and screwed around, said yeah, this is no uglier than anyone else's." Once again players resisted the styling and the imposed Japanese origin of the Katana, and this guitar too limped on only until 1986.

Japanese Moves

The Japanese operation became Fender's lifeline at this time, providing much-needed product to the company which still had no USA factory. The 1985 Fender catalogue featured an all-Japanese line-up, including the new **Contemporary Stratocasters** and Telecasters which were the first Fenders with the increasingly fashionable heavy-duty vibrato units and string-clamps. Production in Japan was based on a handshake agreement: Fuji would continue to supply Fender with guitars after CBS pulled the plug. Dan Smith estimates that as much as 80 per cent of the guitars Fender sold from late 1984 to the middle of 1986 were made in Japan.

The story of Fender's oriental production is slightly complicated at this stage by the fact that Fuji were not able to make as many guitars as Fender needed. So around 1985 some models began to be made by the Moridaira Musical Instrument Co of Tokyo, which already supplied acoustic guitars to Fender. Smith himself admits confusion when he looks back on this period: "We used part of that for export, and then we bought from Fuji for the USA."

In the midst of this activity, the dollar had started to weaken against other currencies and Fender again had trouble competing on price. So they looked to another of their off-shore acoustic guitar producers, the Young Chang Akki Co of Seoul, South Korea, to make electric guitars. "The product actually was pretty good," Smith remembers of Fender's first fully-fledged Korean guitars, the Squier Standard Strats and Teles, which began to appear in 1985 and lasted around three years (during which time some were also made by Cort in Korea).

Back in the United States Fender had finally established their new factory at Corona, about 20 miles east of the now defunct Fullerton site. Production started on a very limited scale toward the end of 1985 when they were building only about five guitars per day for the Vintage re-issue series. But Dan Smith and his colleagues wanted to re-establish the USA side of Fender's production with some good, basic Strats and Teles that

Fender ad 1991 *(above)*
This advertisement in a Japanese music magazine flies the flag for the US Fender company, promoting the Clapton and Malmsteen signature Strats.

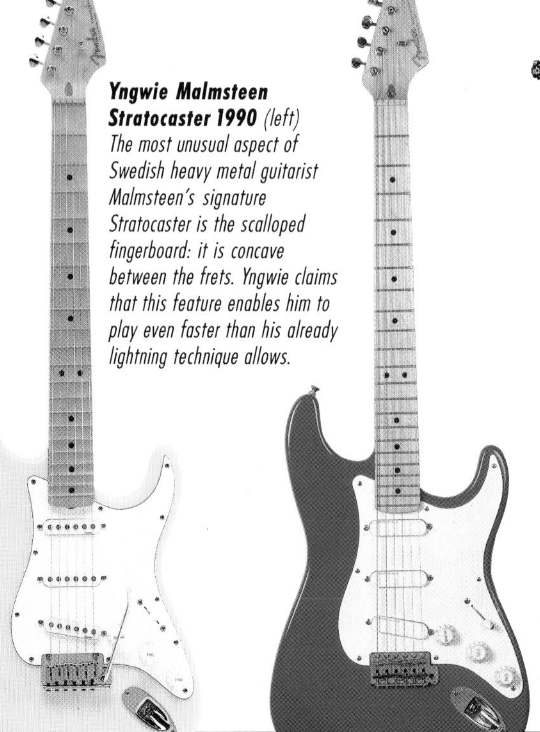

Yngwie Malmsteen Stratocaster 1990 *(left)*
The most unusual aspect of Swedish heavy metal guitarist Malmsteen's signature Stratocaster is the scalloped fingerboard: it is concave between the frets. Yngwie claims that this feature enables him to play even faster than his already lightning technique allows.

Eric Clapton Stratocaster 1990 *(left)*
This was the first of Fender's signature guitars, launched in 1988. Clapton is among the best-known guitarists in the world, having built on blues-based 1960s roots to achieve a more conventional and successful rock career in the 1980s and 1990s. The Clapton Strat uses modern Lace pickups linked to an active circuit, and features Eric's favoured blocked-off vintage-style vibrato.

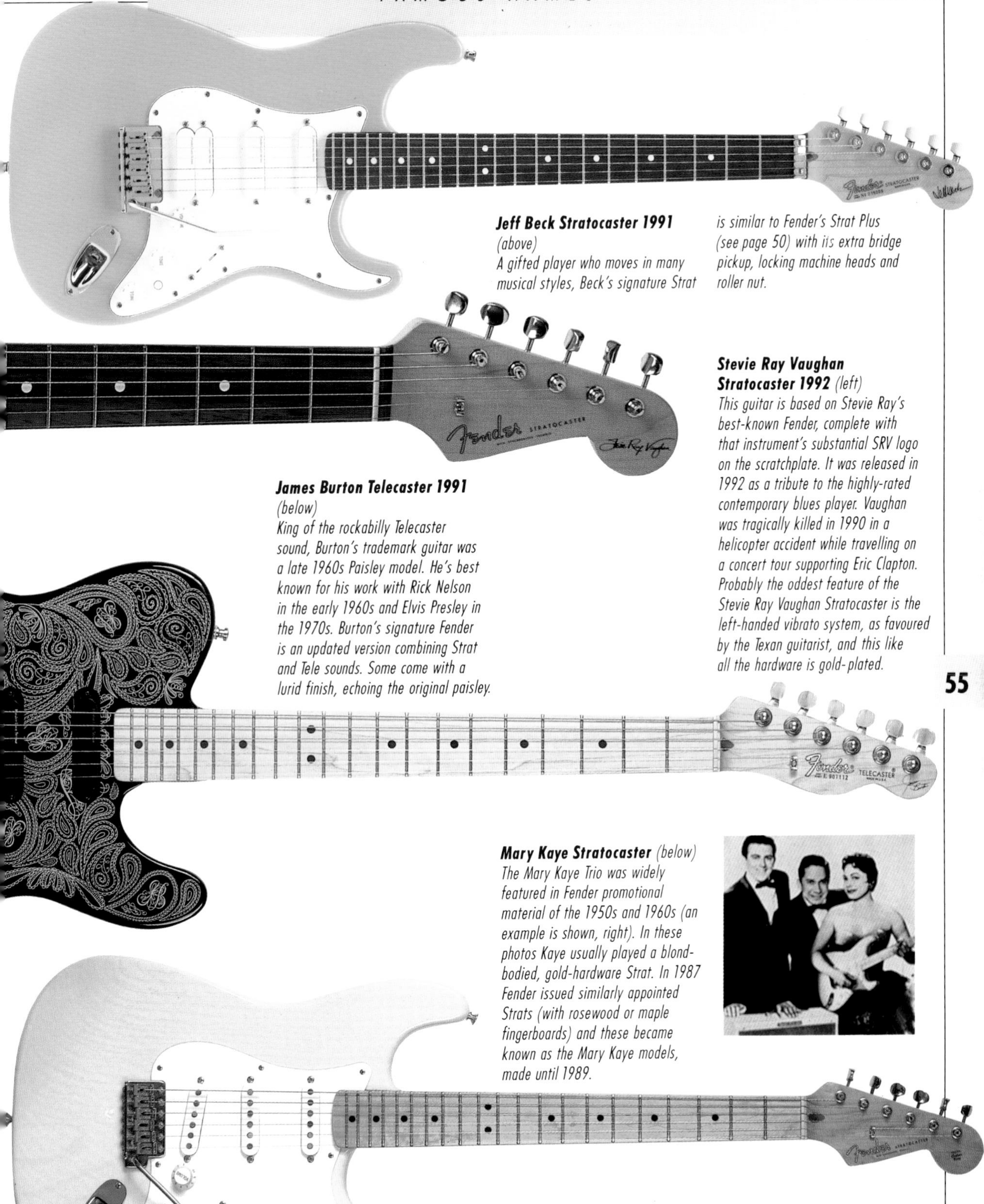

Jeff Beck Stratocaster 1991 *(above)*
A gifted player who moves in many musical styles, Beck's signature Strat is similar to Fender's Strat Plus (see page 50) with its extra bridge pickup, locking machine heads and roller nut.

Stevie Ray Vaughan Stratocaster 1992 *(left)*
This guitar is based on Stevie Ray's best-known Fender, complete with that instrument's substantial SRV logo on the scratchplate. It was released in 1992 as a tribute to the highly-rated contemporary blues player. Vaughan was tragically killed in 1990 in a helicopter accident while travelling on a concert tour supporting Eric Clapton. Probably the oddest feature of the Stevie Ray Vaughan Stratocaster is the left-handed vibrato system, as favoured by the Texan guitarist, and this like all the hardware is gold-plated.

James Burton Telecaster 1991 *(below)*
King of the rockabilly Telecaster sound, Burton's trademark guitar was a late 1960s Paisley model. He's best known for his work with Rick Nelson in the early 1960s and Elvis Presley in the 1970s. Burton's signature Fender is an updated version combining Strat and Tele sounds. Some come with a lurid finish, echoing the original paisley.

Mary Kaye Stratocaster *(below)*
The Mary Kaye Trio was widely featured in Fender promotional material of the 1950s and 1960s (an example is shown, right). In these photos Kaye usually played a blond-bodied, gold-hardware Strat. In 1987 Fender issued similarly appointed Strats (with rosewood or maple fingerboards) and these became known as the Mary Kaye models, made until 1989.

would be seen as a continuation of the best of Fender's American traditions. That plan translated into the **American Standard** models: the Strat was launched in 1986 and the Tele followed two years later.

"When we started the American Standard thing we didn't have any money," Smith recalls, "so we sat down and said we need to come up with a real basic, straightahead Stratocaster." The team had learned from mistakes like the Elite vibrato that the focus had to be on simplicity. "We know that makes it work better, and that's what we did."

The American Standard was an efficacious piece of re-interpretation. It drew from the best of the original Stratocaster but was updated with a flatter-camber 22-fret neck and a revised vibrato unit based on twin-stud pivot points. Once the Corona plant's production lines reached full speed the American Standard Strat proved extremely successful for the revitalised Fender company, and by the early 1990s the guitar was a best-seller notching up some 25,000 sales annually.

LACE AND WILKINSON

For a year or two the American Standard Strat was offered in a Deluxe version, fitted with Fender's special pickups, the so-called Lace Sensor units. Don Lace, an expert in magnetics, had tried to interest Fender in his designs before the CBS sale, and discussions reopened afterwards. Lace's original idea was for a bass pickup, but Fender said that their main requirement was for a new guitar pickup. They wanted to continue in the direction started with the Elite pickups, aiming for the ideal of a low-noise pickup with low magnetic attraction which still delivered the classic single-coil sound. These requirements resulted in the Lace Sensor pickups. While not to every player's taste, they are a viable alternative to Fender's standard pickup designs, and have been offered on various models since 1987.

The **Strat Plus** launched in that year was the first Fender to carry the Lace Sensors, and it also introduced to Fender customers Trev Wilkinson's 'roller-nut,' designed to reduce friction at the nut when using the vibrato. Wilkinson, an Englishman who settled in California, had at first offered his standard roller unit, but Fender asked him to come up with a nut featuring double rollers for each string – as eventually used on the Strat Plus and other Fenders. "The only problem we've had with this," says Dan Smith, "is an occasional buzzing from the nut. But Trev's continually trying to work that out, as are we. And all the guitars that use it have been very successful for us."

Also in 1987 Fender officially established their Custom Shop at the Corona plant. This operation, now separate from the main factory, was started so that Fender could build one-offs and special orders for players with the money and the inclination. It now also produces limited runs of specific models (including some of the company's 'signature' models based on the Fenders used by famous players) which are deemed unsuitable for production in the main plant, usually because the run is too small or the guitar is too specialised.

The Custom Shop grew from Fender's intention, post-CBS, to have a very small production facility in California. "We were only going to make ten Vintage pieces a day," Smith recalls, "so we were going to start a Custom Shop to build special projects for artists, to make certain that the prestige was still there for the company."

Custom guitar builder George Blanda was originally recruited for that purpose in 1985, but a year later, when shifting exchange rates began to favour exports, demand for USA-made product increased dramatically. Fender needed an R&D specialist to come up with new models and the job fell to Blanda: he had the perfect combination of an engineering capability and a love of guitars. But of course this move by Blanda left the Custom Shop position vacant. So Fender then discussed the idea with various guitar makers including Michael Stevens and John Carruthers, and also with former Fender R&D man John Page, who had left the company a year earlier to concentrate on his music. The result was that Stevens and Page joined Fender to start the Custom

Shop in January 1987. Three years later the Custom Shop and Fender R&D were merged.

One of the first jobs for the Custom Shop was to make a yellow Vintage re-issue Strat for Jeff Beck. At this stage Beck vetoed Fender's wish to produce a Jeff Beck signature edition Strat, and the design originally intended for that purpose evolved into the Strat Plus. A Jeff Beck signature Strat not dissimilar to the Plus finally appeared in 1991.

SELLING A SIGNATURE

The first signature guitar produced by Fender was the **Eric Clapton Stratocaster**. Clapton had asked Fender to make him a guitar with the distinct V-shaped neck of his favourite 1930s Martin, and with what he described to Dan Smith as a "compressed" pickup sound. Various prototypes were built by George Blanda, and the final design eventually went on sale in 1988. Lace Sensor pickups and an active circuit delivered the sound Clapton was after, and curiously the production model even has a blocked-off vintage-style vibrato unit, carefully duplicating that feature of Clapton's original.

A number of general production signature models have followed, each endowed with features favoured by the named artist. Stratocasters include the **Yngwie Malmsteen** (with scalloped fingerboard), **Robert Cray** (no vibrato) and **Stevie Ray Vaughan** (left-handed vibrato). Telecasters too have their famous friends, with signature editions such as the **Albert Collins** (with neck humbucker), **Danny Gatton** (Joe Barden twin-blade pickups) and **Jerry Donahue** (Strat neck pickup). Probably the best-known Fender Telecaster player, **James Burton**, was duly honoured by a Fender signature edition in 1990. The new model combines a Telecaster and Stratocaster, incorporating three Lace Sensor pickups and a five-way selector. Finishes include a modern translation of the paisley of Burton's late 1960s Tele.

In 1988 the Custom Shop produced the **40th Anniversary Telecaster**, its first limited-edition production run. At that time, most people including Fender themselves believed that the first Broadcaster/ Telecaster had been produced in 1948, hence the timing of the anniversary model. "When we started making the Anniversary Teles in June 1988," remembers John Page of the Custom Shop, "we had grown from two to four people. We had announced this Tele as a limited edition of 300 guitars, and it was like: oh my god! How are we going to do this?" Beautiful figured maple was used for the body face of the 40th Anniversary Tele, and obtaining such fine wood in sufficient quantity was a new problem for the Custom Shop. Page reports that it took some 18 months to build the full edition of 300 guitars, "and then a lot of dealers were real upset because we only released 300."

So the Shop's next limited run, the **HLE Stratocaster** (Haynes Limited Edition), was upped to 500 units. Page remembers calling a lot of guitar collectors and dealers to ask what they would like to see in a limited edition run, and many nominated the gold-finished 1950s Strat as used by Homer Haynes of musical duo Homer & Jethro. "We borrowed the original, spec'd it out, and released it in 1989," says Page.

Other limited runs continue to appear from the Custom Shop, and this has become an increasingly important part of the Shop's role within the company. In the early 1990s the Custom Shop was building between 2000 and 3000 guitars a year, consisting not only of limited production runs but also custom one-offs – the other strand of the Shop's business. Naturally these one-offs can be of any type and specification, but Page identifies three broad groups among his customers' individual orders: absolute vintage reproductions with spot-on accuracy to satisfy the most nit-picking Fender-obsessed collector; 'quasi-exact' reproductions of classic Fenders "where the guy doesn't necessarily want to be exact, he wants it to be close and he wants that vibe, but he wants a fatter neck, hotter pickups and so on"; and last, the pure one-off fantasy guitar.

"The sky's the limit with those," estimates Page, who gives a few examples: luxuriously appointed 'Rolls Royce'

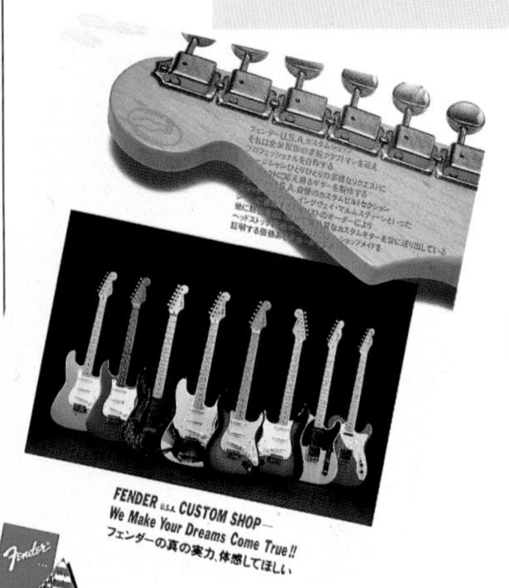

Fender Japan ad 1990 *(above)*
A good deal of the Custom Shop's business comes from Japan, and this advertisement from a Japanese magazine promotes the Shop's services, with the apposite phrase 'We make your dreams come true'.

'Knebworth' Telecaster 1990 *(below)*
This is an example of a Custom Shop one-off, made for the Nordoff-Robbins music therapy charity. The Telecaster-based guitar, seen here in its original state, was later signed by a host of music stars who played at a special benefit concert, and was then sold at auction in aid of the charity. Despite Fender's unwritten rule to leave their standard headstock designs unmodified, Custom Shop man John Page says that an exception was made to incorporate the Nordoff-Robbins logo into the guitar's design.

HLE Stratocaster 1989 *(above)*
Fender's Custom Shop personnel had considered a number of options for their second limited production run instrument. After consulting various guitar collectors and dealers, they came up with this Homer Haynes Limited Edition model. It is based on the 1950s Strat once owned by Haynes, and features an attractive all-gold finish complemented by gold-plated hardware. The Custom Shop produced the HLE in a run of 500 instruments.

Danny Gatton Telecaster 1991 *(left)*
After the Custom Shop made a duplicate of ace guitarist Danny Gatton's old Telecaster, a production run was started and the result is this signature edition. It's an updated version of Gatton's vintage guitar.

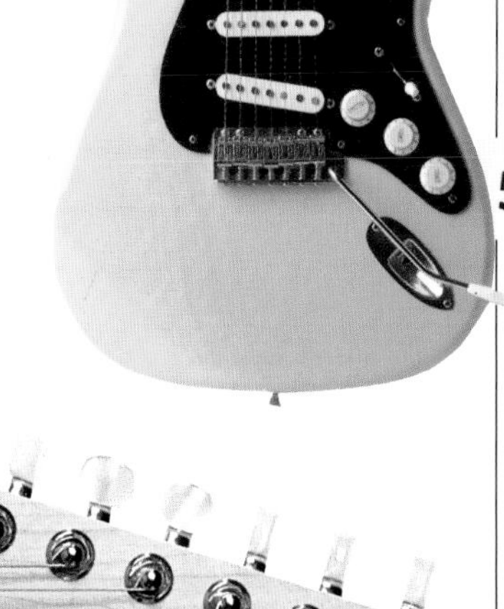

Seven-string prototype 1992 *(right)*
Prototypes of a seven-string Alex Gregory signature Stratocaster were made in 1987. This second Custom Shop prototype was built five years later.

Custom Shop 1990 *(above)*
Guitar-maker Fred Stuart is one of several employed at Fender's Custom Shop. He is pictured at his workbench in the main Shop, housed in a building separate from the Fender factory in Corona.

Hank Marvin Stratocaster 1990 *(below)*
This small-quantity production model with active circuity predates the official signature version which was planned for release in 1992.

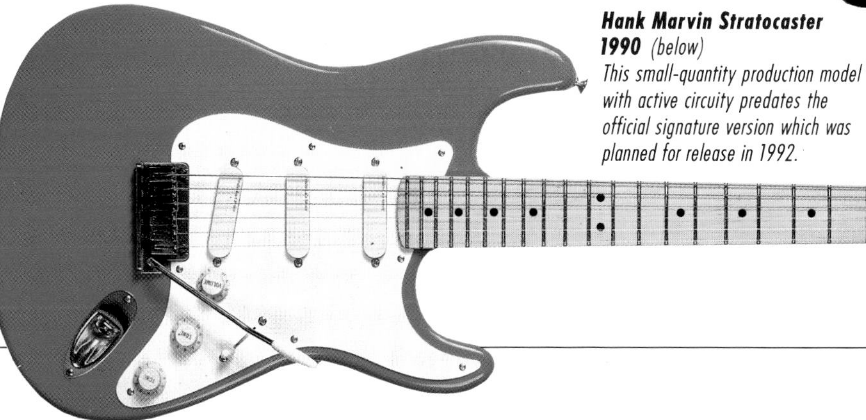

versions of tradition-based guitars; 30in-scale Telecasters; eight-string Strats; and weirdos like "a three-tone Jazzmaster that looked like a 1950s Oldsmobile" or an electric banjo with pedal steel footpedals. But such outlandishly peculiar orders are rare, as Dan Smith says: "As far as I can remember we haven't had to make any Bananacasters. To tell the truth it's almost a disappointment, it was something we did think we'd get. But they take that stuff to someone like Hamer or Jackson or whoever. We seem to get the guys who pretty much want a traditional thing done weird."

Another reason for the establishment of the Custom Shop was to give Fender the opportunity to test out a guitar made in small quantities, to see whether it might become a successful full-production model. Dan Smith: "In my mind, for Fender to continue to be a growing, viable, innovative company, we need about 85 to 90 per cent of our product to be reactive to the market, to be what people want. But there's got to be space for 10 or 15 per cent of it where we can screw around a little bit and see what's maybe going to come next."

The Custom Shop has proved to be a firm success for the new Fender company. It can give players a more personal contact with a major manufacturer, and provides the ideal facility for exploring new ideas both from within and without the Fender organisation.

METAL MANIA

The Fender Japan **HRR Strat**, launched in 1990, was just such a development. It's essentially a vintage-style Stratocaster topped with a locking vibrato, a powerful 'hot' humbucking pickup in the bridge position and a very slim neck. That was a distillation of the requests the Custom Shop was receiving from younger heavy metal-inclined players, and with the USA facility already at peak capacity the guitar was made by Fender Japan. "On the other hand," says Smith, "we had the players who were 25 and older, the Richie Samboras and numerous other guys who'd been playing for a while, and their request was for a really straightahead vintage-type guitar, but with a Floyd Rose locking vibrato, non-recessed bridge cavity, thicker neck, and a PAF-type humbucker at the bridge." That general request turned into the **Floyd Rose Classic Stratocaster**, which became available in 1992.

Floyd Rose, a guitar hardware designer best known for his heavy-duty locking vibrato system, joined forces with Fender toward the end of 1991. Fender acquired the exclusive rights to Floyd Rose products bearing his name. Other makers can still buy licensed hardware, but Fender now have access to Rose's sharp design skills as well as the assistance that his name brings in selling to the heavy metal market. To these guitarists 'Floyd Rose' has become almost synonymous with the heavy-duty locking vibratos so closely associated with the fast, highly technical style of playing which reached a peak of popularity in the early 1990s. "We realise that the market is tailing off for that," admits Smith, "but long term, if we really want to be part of that market, I think Floyd is a good guy to have on board. And actually just from signing him we've attracted a lot of players that we didn't have before."

SET NECKS AND COLLECTIBLES

Fender had decided to have another stab at Gibson-style glued-neck guitars in 1990, when the Custom Shop began to make the **Set Neck Telecaster**. A Stratocaster version followed in 1992, and the guitars were given the fashionably smooth 'heel-less' joint at the junction of neck and body. Time will tell if this latest glued-neck Fender will succeed where the Japanese Master Series failed. At least the Set-neck models have the advantage of Strat and Tele styling.

Following the success of the Vintage re-issue series introduced in 1982, Fender Japan have marketed a growing number of models re-creating many of the guitars from Fender's past. These have included reproductions of the Paisley, Blue Flower, Rosewood and Thinline Telecasters, the Jaguar and Jazzmaster, the Mustang, and of course Strats of various periods. In 1992

Fender USA came up with the term 'Collectibles' to cover many of these instruments that would now be made available for export on a special-order basis only. Separate from their export business, Fender Japan still produce guitars for sale solely in Japan.

Having effectively met the challenge of 'copy' guitars by establishing their own Japanese company, Fender have been active during recent years in defending their trademarks. Dan Smith remembers one particular example of the attitude of some eastern makers. "We went to a store in Korea and every electric guitar was called Fender: they would say Charvel Fender, Gibson Fender – 'Fender' meant 'electric guitar'. They think it's their birthright, you know? What's yours is theirs and what's theirs is theirs."

But Fender have been most concerned about the illegal use of their headstock design, principally the classic Strat outline. Smith: "CBS had applied for trademark rights on the headstocks, and they were granted. The proof for that is not necessarily who did them first, but who's most famous for it. And we've been defending those trademarks since we arrived. Problem is we couldn't actually get them in a lot of countries around the world, because everybody's laws are a little bit different. We can't stop the use of the headstock in Europe, for example, but we are protected in the USA, where nobody should sell a guitar using our head."

Smith estimates that there have probably been as many as 30 actions since he joined Fender in 1981. "On average over the last ten years we've probably spent two or three million dollars protecting trademarks. Now if that had been spent on product development or advertising or artist relations or something . . . '

Prodigious Mexicans

Fender USA came up with a new design in 1991 called the **Prodigy**, an attempt to compete with successful guitars from popular makers of the time such as Ibanez and Charvel. It has an offset-waist body with sharper horns than a Strat, two single-coils and a humbucker, and optional locking vibrato. The Prodigy was among the first Fenders to receive attention at the company's new factory in Mexico, which had been set up in 1990. With a guitar like the Prodigy effectively being produced in two places – some work was done in the USA, some in Mexico – Fender take advantage of an American Customs guideline that the official country of a product's manufacture can be determined by its 'last place of major transformation', together with a consideration of the place where the greater percentage of its value is added. The Prodigy is thus officially 'Made In USA', notwithstanding Mexican assistance, while the Standard Stratocaster of the early 1990s, for example, is 'Made In Mexico', despite contributions from the USA plant.

By early 1992 the Mexican factory was producing around 175 Fender Standard Stratocasters per day, and the plan is eventually to use the facility to make all Fender's budget-priced guitars. "It's great for us," says Smith, "because it's only about three hours from Corona: it's our people, it's our plant, and that's really the way it should be done." The chief advantage of such foreign production sites is the cheapness of the labour, and Fender have like many western companies searched far and wide for this expediency. The company used an Indian factory during 1989 and 1990, but gave up quickly. "It's an incredibly difficult place to get anything decent from," reckons Smith. Over the years Fender had also considered production sources in the former East Germany, Yugoslavia, Czechoslovakia, and many other countries throughout the world.

The Fender Musical Instruments Corporation of the 1990s is well aware of the value of its founder's surname. But many musicians, collectors and guitar dealers measure the worth of Fender purely in terms of past achievements – a frustration for a modern company whose new ideas are often resisted for being 'un-Fender'. Fender's history has been a remarkable mixture of inspiration, luck and mishap, but the best of the resulting guitars will ensure that the Fender name lives on for many years to come.

Fender Japan ad 1991 *(above)*
Fender Japan have always made a comprehensive range of guitars specifically for their home market, including short-scale and medium-scale versions of favourites like the Strat. The short-scale version was introduced to other countries in the late 1980s.

Strat XII 1990 *(right)*
Only the second production 12-string electric from Fender, this first appeared in 1988 and was still in the catalogue in 1992, despite having apparently missed another of the periodic phases of fashion for twelves. The bridge has strong echoes of the company's Electric XII model of the mid-1960s (see page 26) but the headstock is a new design and the rest of the appointments are very Strat-like.

Performer 1986 *(right)*
This impressive guitar had a radically different body design for Fender and a pointed headstock based on the 1969 Swinger design (see page 34). The combination of these design elements with a 24-fret neck was intended to compete with the newly popular 'superstrat' guitars from makers like Jackson. But the Performer, launched in 1985, lasted only until the following year. It was a victim of the uncertainty surrounding the sale of Fender by CBS, and the cool reaction of some players to a Japanese guitar.

Fender Japan ad 1992 *(left)*
The Custom Shop limited edition guitar in this Japanese music press ad celebrates the 10th anniversary of the foundation of Fender Japan in 1982. The company was started so that Fender could make and sell guitars in the domestic Japanese market – a means of countering the burgeoning oriental production of copies of Fender's most famous guitars.

Squier Hank Marvin Stratocaster 1992 *(right)*
Production of Fender's Squier brand had been moved from Japan to Korea in 1988, but in 1992 the marque was again applied to Japanese-made guitars. The new ranges include a basic line called the Silver Series, and this red Strat endorsed by Shadows guitarist Hank Marvin who has long been associated with the US-made original instrument.

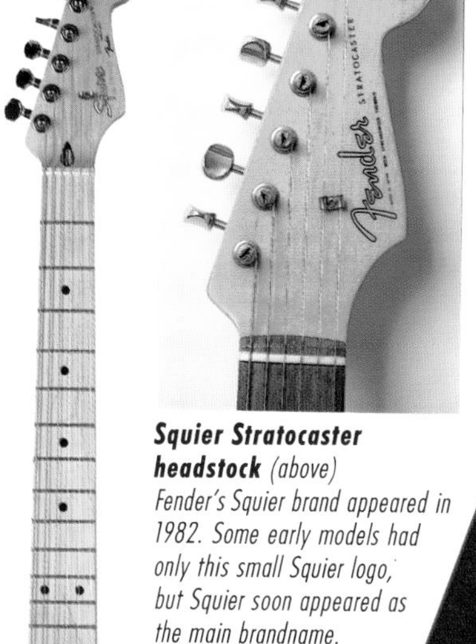

Squier Stratocaster headstock *(above)*
Fender's Squier brand appeared in 1982. Some early models had only this small Squier logo, but Squier soon appeared as the main brandname.

QUALITY BEGINS WITH SQUIER STRINGS

Squier strings are used as original equipment by more manufacturers of instruments than any other American made strings. Packaged as Esquier and Concert Master strings. Available from your favorite music store.

Since 1890 "a string to remember"

V.C. SQUIER CO. BATTLE CREEK, MICHIGAN

V C Squier ad 1960s *(above)*
The string-making company of V C Squier ('a string to remember') was acquired by CBS when they owned Fender. Years later the name was revived for Fender's budget range of Japanese-made instruments.

Esprit: Homage To The Past, An eye To The Future

Fender catalogue 1984 *(above)*
The electric Master Series included semi-solid Esprit and Flame models and the archtop D'Aquisto, designed to compete with Gibson guitars. This page shows the symmetrically cutaway body of the Esprit.

Katana 1985 *(above)*
Fender tried to compete with the odd-shape guitars of other makers by concocting this peculiar design in 1985, but it proved to be unsuccessful and lasted only another year.

REFERENCE SECTION

There are three parts within the reference section that takes up the rest of this book. On pages 68 and 69 is a CHRONOLOGY showing all the electric guitars made by Fender in the order that they were introduced. Starting on page 70 is the main REFERENCE LISTING of Fender models, in alphabetical order, and this is analysed in detail below. Closing the reference section on pages 91-93 is an explanation of the methods that can be used for DATING Fender guitars.

The main Reference Listing (pages 70-90) uses a simple, condensed format to convey a large amount of information about every Fender model, and the following notes are intended to ensure that you gain the most from this unique inventory.

The list covers all electric models issued by Fender USA between April 1950 and May 1992, and the export models of Fender Japan issued since 1982 and until May 1992. As in the rest of this book, there are no acoustic guitars, bass guitars or steel guitars. The four main sections of the list are: 1 Fender – USA; 2 Fender – Japan; 3 Squier – Japan; 4 Other Countries.

Each guitar is listed by the alphabetical order of its model name. Where a model name is also a person's name, the first word still supplies the alphabetical order – for example, the Eric Clapton Stratocaster is listed under E, the Floyd Rose Classic Stratocaster under F, and so on. The only exception to alphabetical order is found under 'Standard' Stratocaster and Telecaster groupings in the USA section. These are listed in chronological order for ease of reference.

At the head of each entry is the model name in bold type, followed by a date or range of dates showing the production period of the instrument. It is worth stressing here the approximate nature of these dates. In many cases it is virtually impossible to pinpoint with total accuracy the period during which a model was in production at the factory. Fender's promotional catalogues usually bear dates, but the content was often decided far in advance and does not always reflect what was being made when the catalogue was eventually issued. Similarly, Fender's dated pricelists itemise the models that the company were selling at any one time, and not necessarily the guitars that were then in production. Naturally we have gone to some lengths to list the most accurate dates possible – but please treat them as approximate, because that is all they can be.

In italics, following the model name and production dates, is a brief, one-sentence identification of the guitar in question. This is intended to help you recognise a specific model at a glance. To enable you to do this we have noted elements of the guitar's design that are unique to that particular model.

Under these opening lines is a body shape number in a panel. This refers to one of the numbered body silhouettes ranged along the bottom of the page, providing an instant illustration of the specific outline used for that model.

For some guitars there may be a sentence below the body shape panel reading 'Similar to . . . except:' or 'As . . . except:'. This will refer to another model entry. The points that follow list any differences between the two models.

In most guitar entries there will be a series of points listed under the body shape panel. To avoid repetition, we have considered a number of features to be common to all Fender models. They are:

Metal tuner buttons unless stated.
Standard Fender headstock shapes unless stated.
Four-screw neckplate unless stated.
Bolt-on neck unless stated.
25.5in-scale, 21 frets unless stated.
Fingerboard with dot markers unless stated.
Solid, contoured, double-cutaway body unless stated.
Single-coil pickups unless stated.
Nickel- or chrome-plated hardware unless stated.

The list of specification points, separated into groups, provides details of the model's features. In the order listed the points refer to:

- Neck, fingerboard, headstock.
- Body.
- Pickups.
- Controls.
- Scratchplate or pickguard.
- Bridge.
- Hardware finish.

Of course, not every model will need all seven points. Some models were made in a number of variations, and where applicable these are listed (beginning '*Also . . .*') after the specification points, in italics. Any other general comments are made in this position, and guitars produced in the Custom Shop are also identified here.

Some models have only a short listing, all in italics. This is usually because the model is a re-issue or re-creation of an earlier guitar. The listing simply refers to the entry for the original instrument.

All this information is designed to tell you more about your Fender guitar. By using the general information and illustrations earlier in the book combined with the knowledge obtained from the reference section you should be able to build up a very full picture of your instrument and its pedigree.

MODELS & YEARS

This listing shows in chronological order the models introduced by Fender USA, Fender Japan and Squier Japan.

FENDER USA

Broadcaster	1950
Esquire *production model*	1950-69
Telecaster	1951-83
Stratocaster 'pre-CBS'	1954-64
Duo-Sonic *short scale 1st*	1956-64
Musicmaster *short scale 1st*	1956-64
Jazzmaster	1958-80
Custom Esquire *bound*	1959-69
Custom Telecaster *bound*	1959-72
Jaguar	1962-75
Duo-Sonic *short scale 2nd*	1964-69
Duo-Sonic II	1964-69
Musicmaster *short scale 2nd*	1964-69
Musicmaster II/*normal scale*	1964-75
Mustang *normal scale*	1964-81
Mustang *short scale*	1964-69
Electric XII	1965-68
Stratocaster 'CBS Sixties'	1965-71
Coronado I	1966-69
Coronado II	1966-69
Coronado XII	1966-69
Bronco	1967-80
Coronado II Antigua	1967-70
Coronado XII Antigua	1967-70
Coronado II Wildwood	1967-69
Coronado XII Wildwood	1967-69
LTD	1968-74
Montego I	1968-74
Montego II	1968-74
Blue Flower Telecaster	1968-69
Paisley Red Telecaster	1968-69
Thinline Telecaster *1st*	1968-71
Custom/Maverick	1969-70
Rosewood Telecaster	1969-72
Swinger *aka Arrow, Musiclander*	1969
Stratocaster 'CBS Seventies'	1971-81
Thinline Telecaster *2nd*	1971-79
Telecaster Custom *humbucker*	1972-81
Telecaster Deluxe	1973-81
Musicmaster *later type*	1975-80
'Rhinestone' Stratocaster (UK)	1975
Starcaster	1976-80
Lead I	1979-82
Lead II	1979-82
25th Anniversary Stratocaster	1979-80
Strat	1980-83
Black & Gold Telecaster	1981-83
Bullet *1st*	1981-83
Bullet Deluxe	1981-83
Gold/Gold Stratocaster	1981-83
Lead III	1981-82
Stratocaster Standard 1st	1981-83
Strat Walnut	1981-83
Vintage Telecaster	1982-84, 1986-
Vintage '57/'62 Stratocaster	1982-
Bullet *2nd*	1983
Bullet H1/H2/S2/S3	1983
Elite Stratocaster	1983-84
Elite Telecaster	1983-84
Gold Elite Stratocaster	1983-84
Gold Elite Telecaster	1983-84
Stratocaster Standard *2nd*	1983-84
Telecaster Standard	1983-84
Walnut Elite Stratocaster	1983-84
Walnut Elite Telecaster	1983-84
Stratocaster American Standard	1986-
Deluxe Strat Plus	1987-
Mary Kaye '57/'62 Stratocaster	1987-89
Strat Plus	1987-
Eric Clapton Stratocaster	1988-
Telecaster American Standard	1988-
Yngwie Malmsteen Stratocaster	1988-
40th Anniversary Telecaster	1988-90
HLE Stratocaster	1989-90
HM Strat	1989-90
Stratocaster American Standard Deluxe	1989-90
US Contemporary Stratocaster	1989-91
Albert Collins Telecaster	1990-
Danny Gatton Telecaster	1990-
HM Strat Ultra	1990-92
James Burton Telecaster	1990-
Set Neck Telecaster (4 models)	1990-
Telecaster Plus	1990-
US Strat Ultra	1990-
35th Anniversary Stratocaster	1990-91
Jeff Beck Stratocaster	1991-
Deluxe Telecaster Plus	1991-
Prodigy/Prodigy II	1991-
Floyd Rose Classic Stratocaster	1992-
Jerry Donahue Telecaster	1992-
Robert Cray Stratocaster	1992-
Set Neck Stratocaster	1992-

Set Neck Floyd Rose Stratocaster	1992-
Stevie Ray Vaughan Stratocaster	1992-

FENDER JAPAN

Vintage '57/'62 Stratocaster	1982-
Vintage '57 Stratocaster non-vibrato	1982-
'52 Telecaster	1982-
D'Aquisto Elite	1984, 1989-
D'Aquisto Standard	1984
Esprit (3 models)	1984
Flame (3 models)	1984
Contemporary Stratocaster (6 models)	1985-87
Contemporary Telecaster (2 models)	1985-87
Katana	1985-86
Performer	1985-86
Standard '22' Stratocaster	1985-89
'62 Custom Telecaster	1985-
Esquire/Custom Esquire	1986-
Jaguar	1986-
Jazzmaster	1986-
Mustang	1986-
Paisley/Blue Flower Telecaster	1986-
'69 Rosewood Telecaster	1986-
'69 Thinline Telecaster	1986-
'72 Stratocaster	1986-
'72 Telecaster Custom	1986-
'72 Thinline Telecaster	1986-
HM Strat (2 models) *1st*	1988-89
Standard '21'/Special Stratocaster	1988-91
ditto non-vibrato	1988-91
Standard/Special Telecaster	1988-91
Strat XII	1988-
'68 Stratocaster	1988-
'69 Paisley Red Stratocaster	1988-
'69 Blue Flower Stratocaster	1988-
Robben Ford	1989-
Short Scale Stratocaster	1989-
HRR Stratocaster	1990-
Yngwie Malmsteen Stratocaster	1991-
HM Strat *2nd (normal head)*	1991-
HM Strat *3rd (droopy head)*	1991-
HMT Acoustic-Electric Telecaster	1991-
HMT Telecaster (2 models)	1991-
JD Telecaster	1992-

SQUIER JAPAN

Vintage '57/'62 Stratocaster	1982-85
Vintage Telecaster	1982-85
Bullet H2/S3	1983-84
Popular (UK)/'70s (USA) Stratocaster	1983-85
Popular (UK)/'70s (USA) Telecaster	1983-85
Bullet S3T	1985-88
Contemporary Bullet HST	1985-88
Contemporary Stratocaster (3 models)	1985-87
Katana	1985-86
Standard Stratocaster	1985-88
ditto vibrato, locking nut	1985-88
Standard Telecaster	1985-88
Hank Marvin Stratocaster	1992-
Silver Series Stratocaster	1992-
Silver Series Telecaster	1992-

FENDER REFERENCE LISTING: ALL ELECTRIC MODELS 1950-1992

FENDER – USA

'ARROW' See later SWINGER listing.

BROADCASTER *1950 Virtually identical to earliest Telecasters, but "Broadcaster" name on headstock. Some transitional examples have Fender logo only, nicknamed 'No-casters'.*

BRONCO *1967-80 One angled pickup at bridge.*

Body shape 5

- Maple neck with rosewood fingerboard; 24in scale, 22 frets; truss-rod adjuster at body end; plastic tuner buttons (metal from c1975); one string-guide.
- Slab body; red only (black or white from c1975).
- One angled black plain-top pickup (at bridge).
- Two controls (volume, tone) and jack socket, all on scratchplate.
- 13-screw (15-screw from c1970) white (black from c1975) laminated plastic scratchplate.
- Six-saddle bridge/vibrato unit.

BULLET first version *1981-83 'Star' Bullet logo, single cutaway body, six-screw scratchplate.*

Body shape 12

- Fretted maple neck, or maple neck with rosewood fingerboard; truss-rod adjuster at body end; 'star' Bullet logo; one string-guide; Telecaster-style headstock.
- Slab single-cutaway body; red or white.
- Two black or white plain-top pickups (pickup at neck is angled).
- Two controls (volume, tone), three-way selector and jack socket, all on scratchplate.
- Six-screw (plus four at bridge) white or black painted metal scratchplate.
- Six-saddle bridge; raised 'lip' of scratchplate forms tailpiece.

Earliest versions use Korean-made parts (plywood bodies).

BULLET DELUXE *1981-83*

Body shape 12

As BULLET first version, except:
- Eight-screw white or black laminated plastic scratchplate.
- Separate six-saddle bridge with through-body stringing.

BULLET second version *1983*

Body shape 13

As BULLET first version, except:
- Fretted maple neck only.
- Slab body with two offset cutaways.
- Pickups and scratchplate white only.

BULLET H1 *1983*

Body shape 13

As BULLET second version, except:
- One white plain-top humbucker pickup (at bridge).
- Pushbutton coil-tap replacing three-way selector.

BULLET H2 *1983*

Body shape 13

As BULLET H1, except:
- Sunburst and walnut additional finish options.
- Two white plain-top humbucker pickups.

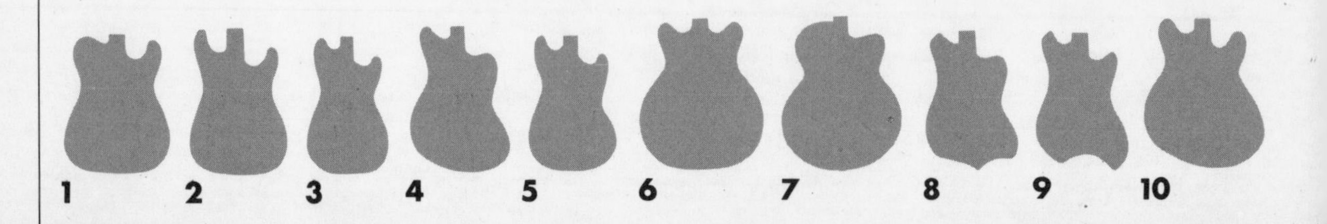

- Three-way selector, plus second pushbutton coil-tap.
- Nine-screw white laminated plastic scratchplate.
- Separate six-saddle bridge with through-body stringing.

BULLET S2 *1983*

Body shape 13

As BULLET DELUXE (see earlier listing), except:
- Fretted maple neck only.
- Slab body with two offset cutaways; sunburst and walnut additional colour options.
- Pickups white only.
- Nine-screw white laminated plastic scratchplate.

BULLET S3 *1983*

Body shape 13

As BULLET S2, except:
- Three white plain-top pickups (pickup at bridge is angled).
- Five-way selector.

CORONADO I *1966-69 Semi-acoustic, long f-holes.*

Body shape 6

- Maple neck with rosewood fingerboard; truss-rod adjuster at body end; plastic tuner buttons; single string-guide.
- Semi-acoustic bound body; sunburst or colours.
- One metal-cover black-centre six-polepiece pickup (at neck).
- Two controls (volume, tone) on body; side-mounted jack socket.
- White or gold laminated plastic pickguard.
- One-saddle wooden bridge, separate tailpiece; or six-saddle metal-top bridge with metal cover, separate vibrato tailpiece.

CORONADO II *1966-69*

Body shape 6

As CORONADO I, except:
- Bound neck, block markers.
- Bound f-holes.
- Two pickups.
- Four controls (two volume, two tone) and three-way selector, all on body.
- Six-saddle metal-top bridge with metal cover, separate tailpiece with F inlay; or six-saddle all-metal bridge, separate vibrato tailpiece.

Prototypes exist with: unbound dot-marker neck with three-tuners-per-side headstock, truss-rod adjuster at headstock end; unbound body; black laminated plastic pickguard; six-section tailpiece.

CORONADO II ANTIGUA *1967-1970*

Body shape 6

As CORONADO II, except:
- Pearl tuner buttons.
- Special white/brown shaded finish.
- "Antigua" on matching-finish laminated plastic pickguard.
- Vibrato version only.

CORONADO II WILDWOOD *1967-69*

Body shape 6

As CORONADO II, except:
- Pearl tuner buttons.
- Special dye-injected beech body; six different colour combinations.
- "Wildwood" plus I-VI (for colour) on white laminated plastic pickguard.
- Vibrato version only.

CORONADO XII *1966-69*

Body shape 6

As CORONADO II except:
- 12-string version.
- One 'bracket' string-guide; six-tuners-per-side 'hockey stick' headstock.
- Six-saddle metal-top bridge with metal cover, separate tailpiece with F inlay.

CORONADO XII ANTIGUA *1967-70*

Body shape 6

As CORONADO XII, except:
- Pearl tuner buttons.
- Special white/brown shaded finish.
- "Antigua" on matching-finish laminated plastic pickguard.

CORONADO XII WILDWOOD *1967-69*

Body shape 6

As CORONADO XII, except:
- Pearl tuner buttons.
- Special dye-injected beech body; six different colour combinations.
- "Wildwood" plus I-VI (for colour) on white laminated plastic pickguard.

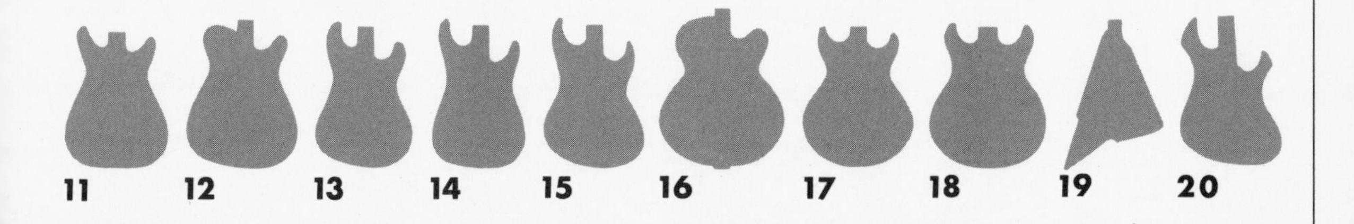

CUSTOM SHOP

The Fender Custom Shop was established in 1987 and has since produced an array of specials, custom-order one-offs and small limited-edition production runs. The latter include the 'Texas Special' Stratocaster and Telecaster, the Bill Carson Stratocaster, the 'unofficial' 1990 Hank Marvin Stratocaster, and the '1960' Esquire, many of which were production runs of 100 or less. Guitars produced by the Custom Shop in larger quantities will be found in the general listing. All Custom Shop instruments carry an appropriate identifying logo on the back of the headstock.

CUSTOM *1969-70 Six-string with 'hockey stick' headstock.*

Body shape 8

▮ Maple neck with bound rosewood fingerboard, block markers; truss-rod adjuster at body end; bracket string-guide on three-tuners-per-side 'hockey stick' headstock.
▮ Offset-waist body with pointed base; sunburst (black back) only.
▮ Two split black plain-top pickups.
▮ Two controls (volume, tone) and jack socket, all on metal plate adjoining scratchplate; four-way selector on scratchplate.
▮ 17-screw tortoiseshell laminated plastic scratchplate.
▮ Six-saddle bridge with metal cover, with vibrato tailpiece.

Some versions have "Maverick", not "Custom", on headstock. Made using modified Electric XII parts; some have purpose-built necks.

DUO-SONIC first version *1956-64 Pickup at neck is angled, pickup at bridge is straight.*

Body shape 3

▮ Fretted maple neck (maple neck with rosewood fingerboard from c1959); 22.5in scale, 21 frets; truss-rod adjuster at body end; plastic tuner buttons; one string-guide.
▮ Slab body; originally beige only; later sunburst or colours.
▮ Two plain-top pickups (pickup at neck is angled).
▮ Two controls (volume, tone), three-way selector and jack socket, all on scratchplate.
▮ Eight-screw anodised metal scratchplate (12-screw white or tortoiseshell laminated plastic from c1960).
▮ Three-saddle bridge/tailpiece with metal cover.

DUO-SONIC second version/DUO-SONIC II *1964-69 Both pickups angled, slide switches above pickups, enlarged headstock.*

Body shape 5

▮ Maple neck with rosewood fingerboard; 22.5in scale/21 frets (Duo-Sonic) or 24in scale/22 frets (Duo-Sonic II); enlarged headstock.
▮ Offset-waist contoured body (early examples with slab body); red, white, or blue.
▮ Two angled white or black plain-top pickups.
▮ Two controls (volume, tone) and jack socket, all on metal plate adjoining scratchplate; two selector slide-switches on scratchplate.
▮ 12-screw pearl or tortoiseshell laminated plastic re-styled scratchplate.
▮ Enlarged three-saddle bridge/tailpiece.

ELECTRIC XII *1965-68 Twelve-string with 'hockey-stick' headstock.*

Body shape 4

▮ Maple neck with rosewood fingerboard (bound from c1965), dot markers (blocks from c1966); truss-rod adjuster at body end; one 'bracket' string-guide; six-tuners-per-side 'hockey-stick' headstock.
▮ Offset-waist body; sunburst or colours.
▮ Two split black plain-top pickups.
▮ Two controls (volume, tone) and jack socket, all on metal plate adjoining scratchplate; four-way selector on scratchplate.
▮ 17-screw white or tortoiseshell laminated plastic scratchplate.
▮ 12-saddle bridge with through-body stringing.

ESQUIRE *1950-69 Single cutaway, one pickup.*

Body shape 1

■ Fretted maple neck (rosewood fingerboard from c1959; maple fingerboard option officially from c1967, replaced by fretted maple neck c1969); truss-rod adjuster at body end (very few earliest examples without truss-rod); one string-guide.
■ Slab single-cutaway body; originally blond only, later sunburst or colours.
■ One angled black six-polepiece pickup (in bridge plate).
■ Two controls (volume, tone) and three-way selector, all on metal plate adjoining scratchplate; side-mounted jack socket.
■ Five-screw black plastic scratchplate (white plastic from c1954; eight-screw from c1959; white laminated plastic from c1963).
■ Three-saddle bridge with through-body stringing (strings anchored on bridge plate c1958 only, with no through-body stringing).
Very few earliest examples have second pickup, with metal cover, at neck.
Also CUSTOM ESQUIRE with bound body 1959-69.

JAGUAR *1962-75 Three metal control plates.*

Body shape 4

■ Maple neck with rosewood fingerboard (bound from c1965), dot markers (blocks from c1966); 24in scale, 22 frets; truss-rod adjuster at body end; one string-guide.
■ Offset-waist body; sunburst or colours.
■ Two white six-polepiece pickups, each with metal 'sawtooth' sides.
■ Two controls (volume, tone) and jack socket, all on lower metal plate adjoining scratchplate; selector and two rollers (rhythm volume, rhythm tone), all on upper metal plate adjoining scratchplate; three slide-switches on metal plate inset into scratchplate.
■ Ten-screw white or tortoiseshell laminated plastic scratchplate.
■ Six-saddle bridge with metal cover; spring-loaded string mute; separate vibrato tailpiece.

JAZZMASTER *1958-80 Offset-waist body, two large rectangular pickups.*

Body shape 4

■ Maple neck with rosewood fingerboard (bound from c1965), dot markers (blocks from c1966); truss-rod adjuster at body end; one string-guide.
■ Offset-waist body; sunburst or colours.
■ Two large white (black from c1977) six-polepiece pickups.
■ Two controls (volume, tone), two rollers (rhythm volume, rhythm tone), three-way selector, slide-switch and jack socket, all on scratchplate.
■ Nine-screw anodised metal scratchplate (13-screw white or tortoiseshell laminated plastic from c1959; black laminated plastic from c1976).
■ Six-saddle bridge with metal cover; separate vibrato tailpiece.
Prototypes exist with: fretted maple neck; smaller headstock.

LEAD I *1979-82 Two large metal selector switches near control knobs.*

Body shape 11

■ Fretted maple neck, or maple neck with rosewood fingerboard; truss-rod adjuster at body end; two string-guides.
■ Body sunburst or colours.
■ One black or white 12-polepiece humbucker pickup (at bridge).
■ Two controls (volume, tone), two two-way selectors and jack socket, all on scratchplate.
■ 11-screw black or white laminated plastic scratchplate.
■ Six-saddle bridge with through-body stringing.

LEAD II 1979-82

Body shape 11

As LEAD I, except:
■ Two black or white six-polepiece pickups (both angled).
■ One selector is three-way type.

LEAD III 1981-2
As LEAD I except:
■ Two pickups.
■ Both selectors are three-way types.

LTD *1968-74 Archtop body, pickguard-mounted controls.*

Body shape 7

■ Maple neck with bound ebony fingerboard, 'diamond-in-block' markers; 20 frets; truss-rod adjuster at body end; three-tuners-per-side headstock.

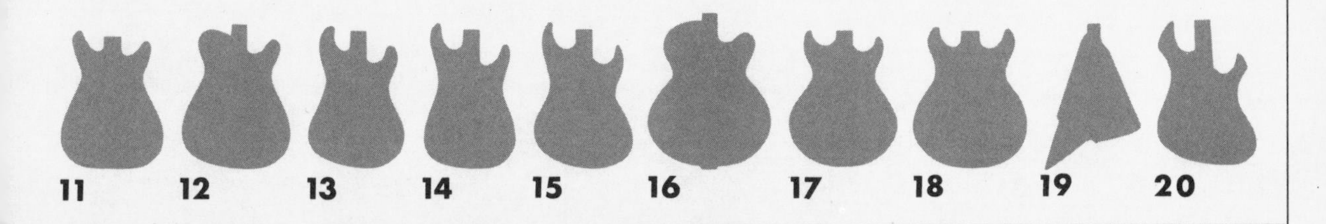

▮ Hollow single-cutaway bound body with carved top; sunburst or natural.
▮ One metal-cover six-polepiece humbucker pickup (neck-mounted via brackets).
▮ Two controls (volume, tone) and jack socket, all on pickguard.
▮ Tortoiseshell laminated plastic pickguard.
▮ One-saddle wooden bridge, separate tailpiece with F inlay.
▮ Gold-plated hardware.

MAVERICK See earlier CUSTOM listing.

MONTEGO I *1968-74 Archtop body, body-mounted controls.*

Body shape 7

▮ Maple neck with bound ebony fingerboard, 'diamond-in-block' markers; 20 frets; truss-rod adjuster at body end; three-tuners-per-side headstock.
▮ Hollow single-cutaway bound body; bound f-holes; sunburst or natural.
▮ One metal-cover six-polepiece humbucker pickup (at neck).
▮ Two controls (volume, tone) on body; side-mounted jack socket.
▮ Black laminated plastic pickguard.
▮ One-saddle wooden bridge, separate tailpiece with F inlay.

MONTEGO II *1968-74*

Body shape 7

As MONTEGO I, except:
▮ Two pickups.

▮ Four controls (two volume, two tone) and three-way selector, all on body.

"MUSICLANDER" See later SWINGER listing.

MUSICMASTER first version *1956-64 One angled pickup at neck.*

Body shape 3

▮ Fretted maple neck (maple neck with rosewood fingerboard from c1959); 22.5in scale, 21 frets; truss-rod adjuster at body end; plastic tuner buttons; one string-guide.
▮ Slab body; originally beige only, later sunburst or colours.
▮ One angled plain-top pickup (at neck).
▮ Two controls (volume, tone) and jack socket, all on scratchplate.
▮ Eight-screw anodised scratchplate (12-screw white or tortoiseshell laminated plastic from c1960).
▮ Three-saddle bridge/tailpiece with metal cover.

MUSICMASTER second version/MUSICMASTER II *1964-75 One angled pickup at neck, controls on metal plate, enlarged headstock.*

Body shape 5

▮ Maple neck with rosewood fingerboard; 22.5in scale/21 frets (Musicmaster) or 24in scale, 22 frets (called II to '69); enlarged headstock.
▮ Offset-waist contoured body (early examples with slab body); red, white, or blue.
▮ One angled white or black plain-top pickup (at neck).
▮ Two controls (volume, tone) and jack socket, all on metal plate adjoining scratchplate.
▮ 12-screw pearl or tortoiseshell laminated plastic re-styled scratchplate.
▮ Enlarged three-saddle bridge/tailpiece.

MUSICMASTER third version *1975-80 One angled pickup at neck, controls on black scratchplate.*

Body shape 5

Similar to MUSICMASTER second version, except:
▮ 24in scale, 22 frets only.
▮ Body black or white.
▮ One angled black plain-top pickup (at neck).
▮ Two controls (volume, tone) on scratchplate.
▮ 15-screw black laminated plastic scratchplate.

MUSTANG *1964-81 Both pickups angled, slide switches above pickups, vibrato tailpiece.*

Body shape 5

F5 Maple neck with rosewood fingerboard; option of 22.5in scale/21 frets or 24in scale/22 frets (24/22 only from c1969); truss-rod adjuster at body end; plastic tuner buttons (metal from c1975); one string-guide (two from c1975); headstock face of 'Competition' version sometimes matches body colour.

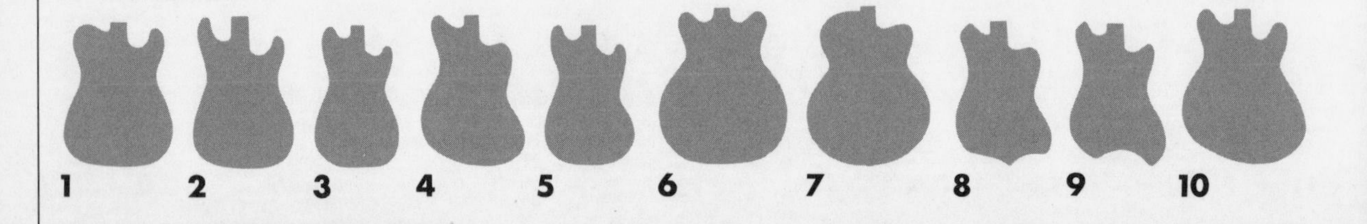

- Offset-waist contoured body (early examples with slab body); sunburst or colours, including 'Competition' body-stripes option (c1968-73).
- Two angled white or black plain-top pickups.
- Two controls (volume, tone) and jack socket, all on metal plate adjoining scratchplate; two selector slide-switches on scratchplate.
- 12-screw pearl or tortoiseshell laminated plastic scratchplate (black laminated plastic only from c1975).
- Six-saddle bridge with vibrato tailpiece.

PRODIGY/PRODIGY II *1991-current Offset-waist body, two single-coils and one humbucker.*

Body shape 15

- Fretted maple neck, or maple neck with rosewood fingerboard; 22 frets; truss-rod adjuster at headstock end; one string-guide (not on II); locking nut on II.
- Offset-waist body; various colours.
- Two black six-polepiece pickups and one black coverless humbucker.
- Two controls (volume, tone), five-way selector and jack socket, all on scratchplate.
- Eight-screw black laminated plastic scratchplate.
- Six-saddle bridge/vibrato unit (locking unit on II).
- Black-plated hardware on II.

REGAL

A range of electric guitars was built in the 1960s for Fender by the Harmony company of Chicago, carrying the Regal brandname on the headstock. Some examples also bear the Fender brandname on the truss-rod cover and an "F" logo on the pickguard.

SQUIER – MADE IN USA

In 1990 and 1991 some USA-made Stratocaster and Telecaster bodies and necks were sent to Fender's Mexican factory for preparation and finishing. They were then returned to the American plant for assembly and completion. This procedure qualified the resulting guitars to carry a 'Made In USA' designation, but they were marketed under the Squier brandname.

STARCASTER *1976-80 Semi-acoustic, black-striped 'hooked' headstock.*

Body shape 10

- Fretted maple neck; 22 frets; 'bullet' truss-rod adjuster at headstock end; one 'bracket' string-guide; three-screw neckplate; black stripe on headstock.
- Semi-acoustic offset-waist bound body with internal centre block; sunburst, natural or colours.
- Two metal-cover six-polepiece humbucker pickups.
- Five controls (two volume, two tone, master volume) and three-way selector, all on body; side-mounted jack socket.
- Black laminated plastic pickguard.
- Six-saddle bridge with through-body stringing.

'Standard' Stratocasters – chronological order

STRATOCASTER 'pre-CBS' *1954-64 Three pickups (angled pickup at bridge), small headstock.*

Body shape 2

- Fretted maple neck (maple neck with rosewood fingerboard from c1959); truss-rod adjuster at body end; one string-guide.
- Body sunburst or colours.
- Three white six-polepiece pickups (pickup at bridge is angled).
- Three controls (one volume, two tone) and three-way selector, all on scratchplate; jack socket in body face.
- Eight-screw white plastic or anodised metal scratchplate (11-screw white or tortoiseshell laminated plastic from c1959).
- Six-saddle bridge with through-body stringing or bridge/vibrato unit with metal cover.

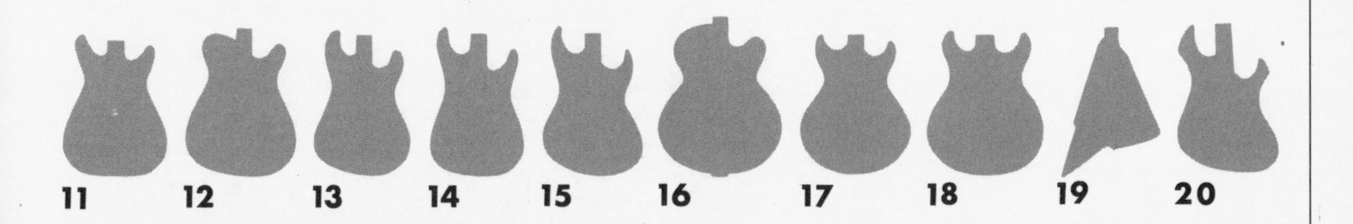

STRATOCASTER 'CBS Sixties' *1965-71*
Enlarged headstock.

Body shape 2

Similar to 'pre-CBS', except:
▮ Maple neck with rosewood fingerboard (small quantity bound) or maple fingerboard option (replaced by fretted maple neck from c1970); enlarged headstock.
▮ 11-screw white or tortoiseshell laminated plastic scratchplate (white laminated plastic only from c1967).
Some early examples have 'pre-CBS'-style small headstock.

STRATOCASTER 'CBS Seventies' *1971-81*
Three-screw neckplate, 'bullet' truss-rod adjuster at headstock end.

Body shape 2

Similar to 'CBS Sixties', except:
▮ Fretted maple neck, or maple neck with rosewood fingerboard; 'bullet' truss-rod adjuster at headstock end; two string-guides; three-screw neckplate.
▮ Pickups white 1971-c75 and c1979-81, and/or black c1975-81.
▮ Five-way selector from c1977.
▮ 11-screw black laminated scratchplate c1975-c81.
Also Antigua version in white/brown shaded finish with matching laminated plastic scratchplate (c1977-79).
Also small number of 'Hendrix' version with left-handed-style 25th Anniversary neck and right-handed 25th Anniversary body with extra contour and finished in white (1980).

STRATOCASTER Standard first version *1981-83*
Small headstock with two string-guides, four-screw neckplate.

Body shape 2

Similar to 'CBS Seventies' except:
▮ Truss-rod adjuster at body end; smaller headstock; four-screw neckplate.
▮ Pickups white only.
▮ 11-screw white laminated plastic scratchplate.

STRATOCASTER Standard second version
1983-84 Two controls, jack socket on scratchplate.

Body shape 2

Similar to Standard first version, except:
▮ Two controls (volume, tone) and jack socket, all on scratchplate.
▮ 12-screw white plastic scratchplate.
▮ Re-designed six-saddle bridge/tailpiece or bridge/vibrato unit.
Also small quantity in red, yellow or blue streaked 'marble' finish (c1984).

STRATOCASTER American Standard *1986-current 22 frets, re-designed vibrato unit.*

Body shape 2

▮ Fretted maple neck, or maple neck with rosewood fingerboard; 22 frets; truss-rod adjuster at headstock end; two string-guides.
▮ Body sunburst or colours.
▮ Three white six-polepiece pickups (pickup at bridge is angled).
▮ Three controls (volume, two tones) and five-way selector, all on scratchplate; jack socket in body face.
▮ 11-screw white laminated plastic scratchplate.
▮ Re-designed six-saddle bridge/vibrato unit.
Also American Standard Deluxe, with three white plain-top Lace Sensor pickups (c1989-90).

Other Stratocasters — A-Z listing

ELITE STRATOCASTER *1983-84 Pushbutton selector switches.*

Body shape 2

▮ Fretted maple neck, or maple neck with rosewood fingerboard; truss-rod adjuster at headstock end; two string-guides.
▮ Body sunburst or colours.
▮ Three white plain-top pickups (pickup at bridge is angled).
▮ Three controls (one volume, two tones) and three pushbutton selectors, all on scratchplate; side-mounted jack socket; active circuit.
▮ 11-screw white laminated plastic scratchplate.
▮ Re-designed six-saddle bridge/tailpiece or bridge/vibrato unit.
Also 'Gold Elite' version with pearl tuner buttons and gold-plated hardware.
Also 'Walnut Elite' version ditto, but with walnut body and neck, ebony fingerboard.

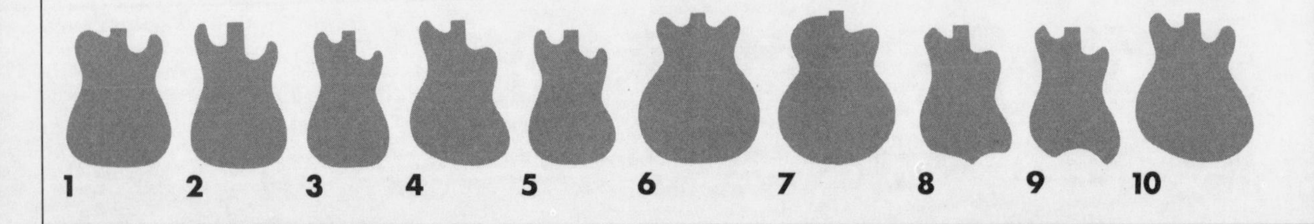

ERIC CLAPTON STRATOCASTER *1988-current Signature on headstock.*

Body shape 2

▮ Fretted maple neck; 21 frets on earliest examples, later 22; truss-rod adjuster at headstock end; one string-guide; Eric Clapton signature on headstock.
▮ Body various colours.
▮ Three white plain-top Lace Sensor pickups (pickup at bridge is angled).
▮ Three controls (volume, two tones) and five-way selector, all on scratchplate; jack socket in body face; active circuit (selected by mini switch on earliest examples).
▮ Eight-screw white plastic scratchplate.
▮ Six-saddle bridge/vibrato unit (blocked off).

FLOYD ROSE CLASSIC STRATOCASTER *1992-current 22 frets, Floyd Rose vibrato, scratchplate has shaped cut-out to match bridge humbucker.*

Body shape 2

▮ Fretted maple neck, or maple neck with rosewood fingerboard; 22 frets; truss-rod adjuster at headstock end; single-bar string-guide; locking nut.
▮ Body sunburst or colours.
▮ Two white six-polepiece pickups and one coverless humbucker (at bridge).
▮ Three controls (volume, two tones) and five-way selector, all on scratchplate; jack socket in body face.
▮ 11-screw white laminated plastic scratchplate.
▮ Six-saddle locking bridge/vibrato unit.

GOLD/GOLD STRATOCASTER *1981-83 Gold body and hardware.*

Body shape 2

Similar to STRAT (see later listing here), except:
▮ Normal "Stratocaster" logo.
▮ Body gold.
▮ Normal controls.
▮ Normal six-saddle bridge/vibrato unit.
▮ Gold-plated hardware.
Small number produced with pearl fingerboard position markers.

HLE STRATOCASTER *1989-90 Gold body, scratchplate and hardware.*

Body shape 2

Similar to VINTAGE '57 (see later listing here), except:
▮ Body gold.
▮ Gold anodised metal scratchplate.
▮ Gold-plated hardware.
Homer Haynes Limited Edition, Custom Shop numbered production run of 500.

HM STRAT (four models) *1989-90 Black headstock with large flamboyant "Strat" logo.*

Body shape 14

▮ Fretted maple neck, or maple neck with rosewood fingerboard; 25.1in scale, 24 frets; truss-rod adjuster at headstock end; flamboyant "Strat" logo; black-faced headstock; locking nut.
▮ Smaller body; various colours.
▮ Black six-polepiece single-coil pickup and/or black coverless humbucker in four layouts: (1) one humbucker; (2) two humbuckers; (3) one single-coil, one humbucker; (4) two single-coils, one humbucker.
▮ Control layouts: (1) volume, tone, coil-tap; (2,3,4) volume, two tones, selector, coil-tap; side-mounted jack socket.
▮ Black laminated plastic scratchplate on one single-coil/one humbucker model; rest no scratchplate.
▮ Six-saddle locking bridge/vibrato unit.
▮ Black-plated hardware.

HM STRAT ULTRA *1990-92 Black headstock with large flamboyant "Strat" logo, triangular fingerboard-markers.*

Body shape 14

Similar to HM STRAT, except:
▮ Ebony fingerboard with split-triangle markers.
▮ Four black plain-top Lace Sensor pickups (two at bridge).
▮ Three controls (volume, two tones), five-way selector, and mini switch between tone controls for either/both selection of two bridge pickups, all on body; side-mounted jack socket.
▮ No scratchplate.
▮ Six-saddle locking bridge/vibrato unit.
▮ Black-plated hardware.

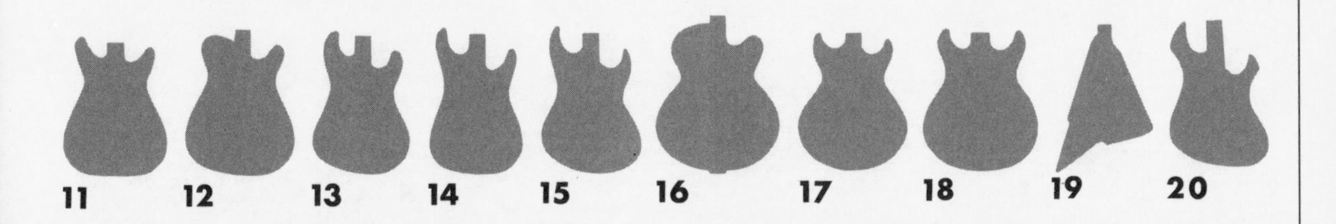

JEFF BECK STRATOCASTER *1991-current Signature on headstock.*

Body shape 2

- Maple neck with rosewood fingerboard; 22 frets; truss-rod adjuster at headstock end; locking machine heads; roller nut; Jeff Beck signature on headstock.
- Body white, green or purple.
- Four white plain-top Lace Sensor pickups (two at bridge).
- Three controls (volume, two tones), five-way selector and switch between tone controls for bridge-pickups selection, all on scratchplate; jack socket in body face.
- 11-screw white laminated plastic scratchplate.
- Re-designed Six-saddle bridge/vibrato unit.

'MARY KAYE' '57 STRATOCASTER *1987-89 Fretted maple neck, see-through blond body finish, gold hardware.*

Body shape 2

As VINTAGE '57 (see later listing here), except:
- Body translucent blond only.
- Gold-plated hardware.

This and the following guitar were named after the artiste who appeared in early Fender literature sporting a 1950s Stratocaster in this finish.

'MARY KAYE' '62 STRATOCASTER *1987-89 Rosewood fingerboard, see-through blond body finish, gold hardware.*

Body shape 2

As VINTAGE '62 (see later listing here), except:
- Body translucent blond only.
- Gold-plated hardware.

'RHINESTONE' STRATOCASTER *1975 Cold-cast bronze body with heavily-carved floral design.*

Body shape 2

As STRATOCASTER 'CBS Seventies', except:
- Replacement body made by British sculptor Jon Douglas, in various colours, some inset with rhinestones.

These were authorised by Fender's UK agent in 1975 and produced in a very small quantity. Unauthorised 1990s versions also exist, and carry an identification plaque on the rear of the body.

ROBERT CRAY STRATOCASTER *1992-current Signature on headstock.*

Body shape 2

- Maple neck with rosewood fingerboard; truss-rod adjuster at body end; one string-guide; Robert Cray signature on headstock.
- Body sunburst, silver or violet.
- Three white six-polepiece pickups (pickup at bridge is angled).
- Three controls (one volume, two tone) and five-way selector, all on scratchplate; jack socket in body face.
- 11-screw white laminated plastic scratchplate.
- Six-saddle bridge/tailpiece.

Custom Shop production.

'SET NECK' STRATOCASTER *1992-current Glued-in neck.*

Body shape 2

Similar to US STRAT ULTRA (see later listing here), except:
- Glued-in neck.

Custom Shop production.

'SET NECK' FLOYD ROSE STRATOCASTER *1992-current Reverse headstock, glued-in neck.*

Body shape 2

- Maple glued-in neck with ebony fingerboard; 22 frets; truss-rod adjuster at headstock end; black-faced reverse headstock; locking nut.
- Smaller body; various colours.
- Two black six-polepiece pickups and one black coverless humbucker (at bridge).
- Two controls (one volume, one tone) and five-way selector, all on body; side-mounted jack socket.
- No scratchplate.
- Six-saddle locking bridge/vibrato unit.
- Black-plated hardware.

Custom Shop production.

STEVIE RAY VAUGHAN STRATOCASTER *1992-current "SRV" on scratchplate.*

Body shape 2

- Maple neck with rosewood fingerboard; truss-rod adjuster at body end; one string-guide; Stevie Ray Vaughan signature on headstock.
- Body sunburst only.

1 2 3 4 5 6 7 8 9 10

■ Three white six-polepiece pickups (pickup at bridge is angled).
■ Three controls (one volume, two tone) and five-way selector, all on scratchplate; jack socket in body face.
■ Eight-screw black laminated plastic scratchplate with "SRV" engraving.
■ Left-handed six-saddle bridge/ vibrato unit.
■ Gold-plated hardware.

STRAT *1980-83 "Strat" logo on headstock, gold knobs.*

Body shape 2

■ Fretted maple neck, or maple neck with rosewood fingerboard; truss-rod adjuster at body end; two string-guides; "Strat" logo on re-styled headstock; headstock face matches colour of body.
■ Body red, blue or white.
■ Three white six-polepiece pickups (pickup at bridge is angled).
■ Three controls (one volume, one tone, one two-way rotary selector) and five-way selector, all on scratchplate; jack socket in body face.
■ 11-screw white laminated plastic scratchplate.
■ Re-designed heavy-duty six-saddle bridge/vibrato unit.
■ Gold-plated brass hardware (early examples have chrome machine heads and polished brass hardware).

STRAT PLUS *1987-current Roller nut, three Lace Sensor pickups.*

Body shape 2

As STRATOCASTER American Standard (see listing in earlier 'Standard' Stratocasters section), except:
■ Roller nut; no headstock string-guides; locking machine heads.
■ Three white plain-top Lace Sensor pickups (pickup at bridge is angled).
Also STRAT PLUS DELUXE version with alternative Lace Sensors.

STRAT WALNUT *1981-83 Walnut body and neck.*

Body shape 2

As STRAT, except:
■ Fretted walnut neck (small quantity with ebony fingerboard).
■ Walnut body.
■ Black laminated plastic scratchplate.
■ Gold-plated hardware.

US CONTEMPORARY STRATOCASTER *1989-91 22 frets, locking vibrato unit, no string-guide.*

Body shape 2

Similar to STRATOCASTER American Standard (see listing in earlier 'Standard' Stratocasters section), except:
■ Maple neck with rosewood fingerboard only; locking nut; no headstock string-guides.
■ Body in colours only.
■ Coverless humbucker (at bridge).
■ Six-saddle locking bridge/vibrato unit.

US STRAT ULTRA *1990-current Four white pickups (two at bridge).*

Body shape 2

Similar to STRAT PLUS (see earlier listing here), except:
■ Ebony fingerboard.
■ Four white plain-top Lace Sensor pickups (two at bridge).
■ Mini-switch between tone controls for either/both selection of two bridge pickups.

VINTAGE '57 STRATOCASTER *1982-current Re-issue based on 1957-period original (see 'pre-CBS' in earlier 'Standard' Stratocasters section).*

VINTAGE '62 STRATOCASTER *1982-current Re-issue based on 1962-period original (see 'pre-CBS' in earlier 'Standard' Stratocasters section).*

YNGWIE MALMSTEEN STRATOCASTER *1988-current Scalloped fingerboard, signature on headstock.*

Body shape 2

■ Fretted maple neck, or maple neck with rosewood fingerboard, both versions scalloped between frets; 21 frets; truss-rod adjuster at body end; two string-guides; brass nut; Yngwie Malmsteen signature on headstock.
■ Body red, white or blue.
■ Three white six-polepiece pickups (pickup at bridge is angled).
■ Three controls (volume, two tones) and five-way selector, all on scratchplate; jack socket in body face.

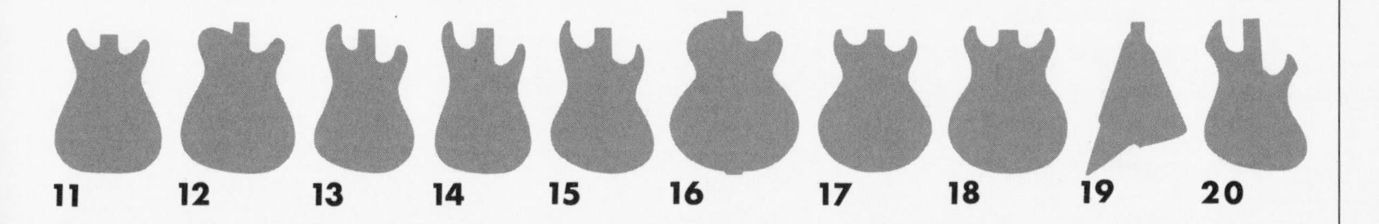

- 11-screw white laminated plastic scratchplate.
- Six-saddle bridge/vibrato unit.

25th ANNIVERSARY STRATOCASTER *1979-80 Anniversary logo on body.*

Body shape 2

Similar to 'CBS Seventies' (see listing in earlier 'Standard' Stratocasters section), except:

- Fretted maple neck only; truss-rod adjuster at body end; commemorative neckplate.
- Body silver (earliest examples pearl white) with "Anniversary" logo.
- Six-saddle bridge/vibrato unit with cover.

35th ANNIVERSARY STRATOCASTER *1990-91 Extra switch between tone controls.*

Body shape 2

Similar to STRATOCASTER American Standard (see listing in earlier 'Standard' Stratocasters section), except:

- Ebony fingerboard.
- Quilted maple body top.
- Three white plain-top Lace Sensor pickups (pickup at bridge is angled).
- Mini switch selects active circuit.

Custom Shop numbered production run of 500.

SWINGER *1969 'Arrow-head'-shaped headstock; 'scooped' body base.*

Body shape 9

- Maple neck with rosewood fingerboard; 22.5in scale, 21 frets; truss-rod adjuster at body end; 'arrow-head' shaped headstock; one string-guide; many have no "Swinger" logo.
- Offset-waist body with 'scoop' in base; various colours.
- One angled black plain-top pickup (at neck).
- Two controls (volume, tone) and jack socket, all on metal plate adjoining scratchplate.
- 12-screw tortoiseshell or pearl laminated plastic scratchplate.
- Three-saddle bridge/tailpiece.

Made from modified Musicmaster/Mustang/Bass-V parts. Also unofficially known as Arrow, or Musiclander.

'Standard' Telecasters – chronological order

TELECASTER *1951-83 Single cutaway, two pickups.*

Body shape 1

- Fretted maple neck 1951-c59 and c1969-83, maple neck with rosewood fingerboard c1959-83, maple fingerboard option c1967-c69; truss-rod adjuster at body end; one string-guide (two from c1972).
- Slab single-cutaway body; originally blond only, later sunburst or colours.
- One plain metal-cover pickup (at neck) and one angled black six-polepiece pickup (in bridgeplate).
- Two controls (volume, tone; earliest versions: volume, pickup blender) and three-way selector, all on metal plate adjoining scratchplate; side-mounted jack socket.
- Five-screw black plastic scratchplate (white plastic from c1954; eight-screw from c1959; white laminated plastic c1963-c75 and c1981-83; black laminated plastic c1975-c81).
- Three-saddle bridge with through-body stringing (strings anchored on bridge plate c1959 only, no through-body stringing); Fender Bigsby bridge and vibrato tailpiece option c1967-c74 (no through-body stringing if factory-fitted).

Also **CUSTOM TELECASTER with bound body** *1959-c72.*

Also special finish versions: Paisley Red and Blue Flower patterns (c1968-69); Antigua in shaded white/brown with matching laminated plastic scratchplate (c1977-79).

TELECASTER Standard *1983-84 Six-saddle bridge with strings anchored on bridge plate.*

Body shape 1

- Fretted maple neck, or maple neck with rosewood fingerboard; truss-rod adjuster at body end; two string-guides.
- Slab single-cutaway body; sunburst or colours.
- One plain metal-cover pickup at neck

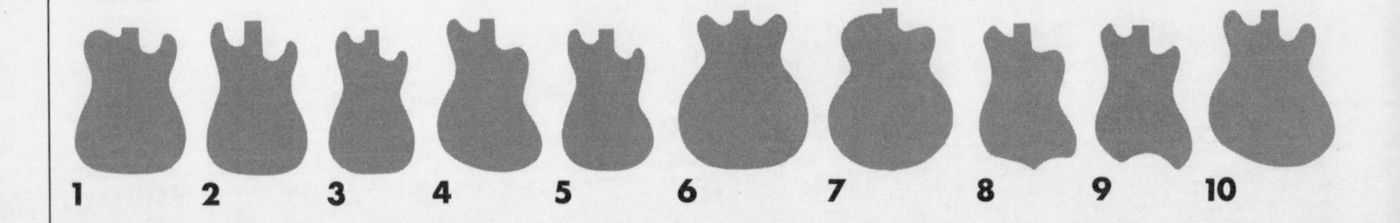

and one angled black six-polepiece pickup (in bridgeplate).
▮ Two controls (volume, tone) and three-way selector, all on metal plate adjoining scratchplate; side-mounted jack socket.
▮ Five-screw white plastic scratchplate (eight-screw on earliest examples).
▮ Re-designed six-saddle lip-less bridge/tailpiece (no through-body stringing).
Also small quantity in red, yellow or blue streaked 'marble' finish (c1984).

TELECASTER American Standard *1988-current 22 frets, six-saddle bridge.*

Body shape 1

▮ Fretted maple neck or maple neck with rosewood fingerboard; 22 frets; truss-rod adjuster at body end; one string-guide.
▮ Slab single-cutaway body; sunburst or colours.
▮ One plain metal-cover pickup with height-adjustment screws visible either side (at neck) and one angled black six-polepiece pickup (in bridgeplate).
▮ Two controls (volume, tone) and three-way selector, all on metal plate adjoining scratchplate; side-mounted jack socket.
▮ Eight-screw white laminated plastic scratchplate.
▮ Re-designed six-saddle lip-less bridge with through-body stringing (earliest examples have raised-lip version).

Other Telecasters – A-Z listing

ALBERT COLLINS TELECASTER *1990-current Metal-cover humbucker at neck, signature on headstock.*

Body shape 1

▮ Maple neck with maple fingerboard; truss-rod adjuster at body end; one string-guide; Albert Collins signature on headstock.
▮ Slab single-cutaway bound body; natural only.
▮ One metal-cover six-polepiece humbucker pickup (at neck) and one angled black six-polepiece pickup (in bridgeplate).
▮ Two controls (volume, tone) and three-way selector, all on metal plate adjoining scratchplate; side-mounted jack socket.
▮ Eight-screw white laminated plastic scratchplate.
▮ Six-saddle raised-lip bridge with through-body stringing.
Custom Shop production.

BLACK & GOLD TELECASTER *1981-83 Black body and headstock, gold hardware.*

Body shape 1

Similar to 1981-style TELECASTER (see listing in earlier 'Standard' Telecasters section) except:
▮ Black headstock face.
▮ Black finish only.
▮ Black laminated plastic scratchplate.
▮ Re-designed heavy-duty six-saddle bridge with through-body stringing.
▮ Gold-plated brass hardware.

DANNY GATTON TELECASTER *1990-current Twin 'blade' pickups, signature on headstock.*

Body shape 1

▮ Fretted maple neck; 22 frets; truss-rod adjuster at body end; one string-guide; Danny Gatton signature on headstock.
▮ Slab single-cutaway body; 'special' finish or gold.
▮ Two black twin-blade pickups (pickup in bridgeplate is angled).
▮ Two controls (volume, tone) and three-way selector, all on metal plate adjoining scratchplate; side-mounted jack socket.
▮ Five-screw cream plastic scratchplate.
▮ Re-designed three-saddle bridge with through-body stringing.
Custom Shop production.

ELITE TELECASTER *1983-84 Two white plain-top pickups.*

Body shape 1

▮ Fretted maple neck, or maple neck with rosewood fingerboard; truss-rod adjuster at headstock end; two string-guides.
▮ Slab single-cutaway bound body; sunburst or colours.
▮ Two white plain-top humbucker pickups.
▮ Four controls (two volumes, two tones) and three-way selector, all on body; side-mounted jack socket; active circuit.
▮ Self-adhesive 'optional' white laminated plastic mini scratchplate.
▮ Re-designed six-saddle bridge/tailpiece.

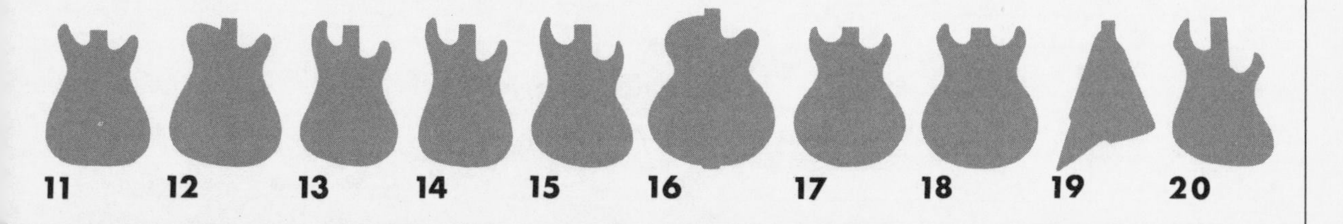

Also 'Gold Elite' version with pearl tuner buttons and gold-plated hardware.
Also 'Walnut Elite' version ditto, but with walnut body and neck, ebony fingerboard.

JAMES BURTON TELECASTER *1990-current No scratchplate, three pickups, signature on headstock.*

Body shape 1

- Fretted maple neck; truss-rod adjuster at body end; one string-guide; James Burton signature on headstock.
- Slab single-cutaway body; white or red, or black with gold paisley or red paisley pattern.
- Three black plain-top Lace Sensor pickups (pickup at bridge is angled).
- Two controls (volume, tone) and five-way selector, all on metal plate; side-mounted jack socket.
- Re-designed six-saddle small bridge with through-body stringing.
- Gold-plated or black-plated hardware.

JERRY DONAHUE TELECASTER *1992-current Black six-polepiece pickup at neck, signature on headstock.*

Body shape 1

- Fretted maple neck; truss-rod adjuster at body end; one string-guide; Jerry Donahue signature on headstock.
- Slab single-cutaway body; sunburst or red.
- Two black six-polepiece pickups (pickup in bridgeplate is angled).
- Two controls (volume, tone) and five-way selector, all on metal plate adjoining scratchplate; side-mounted jack socket.
- Five-screw black laminated plastic scratchplate.
- Three-saddle bridge with through-body stringing.
- Gold-plated hardware.

Custom Shop production.

ROSEWOOD TELECASTER *1969-72 Rosewood body and neck.*

Body shape 1

As late-1960s TELECASTER (see listing in earlier 'Standard' Telecasters section) except:
- Fretted rosewood neck.
- Solid rosewood body (later hollowed).
- Black laminated plastic scratchplate.

SET NECK TELECASTER *1990-current Glued-in neck.*

Body shape 1

- Mahogany glued-in neck with rosewood fingerboard; 22 frets; truss-rod adjuster at headstock end; two string-guides; headstock face and neck matches body colour.
- Semi-solid slab single-cutaway bound body; various colours.
- Two black coverless humbucker pickups.
- Two controls (volume, tone), three-way selector and coil-tap, all on body; side-mounted jack socket.
- Six-saddle small bridge with through-body stringing.

Custom Shop production.

SET NECK TELECASTER COUNTRY ARTIST *1991-current Glued-in neck, gold-plated hardware.*

Body shape 1

Similar to SET NECK TELECASTER, except:
- Angled black six-polepiece pickup (in bridgeplate).
- Small five-screw tortoiseshell laminated plastic scratchplate.
- Re-designed six-saddle lip-less bridge with through-body stringing.
- Gold-plated hardware.

Custom Shop production.

SET NECK TELECASTER PLUS *1990-current. Glued-in neck, vibrato unit.*

Body shape 1

Similar to SET NECK TELECASTER, except:
- Ebony fingerboard; no string-guides; locking machine heads; roller nut.
- Six-saddle bridge/vibrato unit.

SET NECK TELECASTER FLOYD ROSE *1990-current. Glued-in neck, locking vibrato unit.*

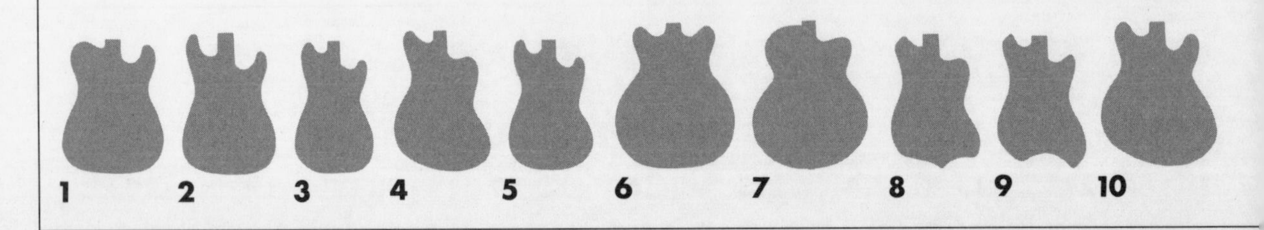

Similar to SET NECK TELECASTER PLUS, except:
▮ Additional central black six-polepiece pickup.
▮ Five-way selector.
▮ Six-saddle locking bridge/vibrato unit.

TELECASTER CUSTOM *1972-81 Humbucker at neck, four controls.*

Body shape 1

▮ Fretted maple neck, or maple neck with rosewood fingerboard; 'bullet' truss-rod adjuster at headstock end; two string-guides; three-screw neckplate.
▮ Slab single-cutaway body; sunburst, natural or colours.
▮ One metal-cover six-polepiece humbucker pickup (at neck) and one angled black six-polepiece pickup (in bridgeplate).
▮ Four controls (two volumes, two tones) and three-way selector, all on scratchplate; side-mounted jack socket.
▮ 16-screw black laminated plastic scratchplate (15-screw on earliest examples).
▮ Six-saddle raised-lip bridge with through-body stringing (three-saddle on earliest examples).
Also Antigua version in white/brown shaded finish with matching laminated plastic scratchplate (c1977-79).
For CUSTOM TELECASTER bound-body version, see TELECASTER listings in earlier 'Standard' Telecasters section.

TELECASTER DELUXE *1973-81 Two humbuckers, Stratocaster-style wide headstock.*

Body shape 1

▮ Fretted maple neck; 'bullet' truss-rod adjuster at headstock end; two string-guides; wide Stratocaster-style headstock; three-screw neckplate.
▮ Contoured single-cutaway body; sunburst, natural or colours.
▮ Two metal-cover six-polepiece humbucker pickups.
▮ Four controls (two volumes, two tones) and three-way selector, all on scratchplate; side-mounted jack socket.
▮ 16-screw black laminated plastic scratchplate.
▮ Six-saddle small bridge with through-body stringing (small quantity with Stratocaster-style six-saddle bridge/vibrato unit).
Also Antigua version in white/brown shaded finish with matching laminated plastic scratchplate (c1977-79).

TELECASTER PLUS *1990-current Three single coils, two together at bridge.*

Body shape 1

Similar to TELECASTER American Standard (see listing in earlier 'Standard' Telecasters section) except:
▮ Three black plain-top Lace Sensor pickups (two in separate surround at bridge).
▮ Additional three-way mini switch giving both/either selection of bridge pickups.
▮ Six-saddle small bridge with through-body stringing.

Also DELUXE TELECASTER PLUS with locking machine heads, roller nut, no string-guide, six-saddle bridge/vibrato unit.

THINLINE TELECASTER first version *1968-71 F-hole body.*

Body shape 1

▮ Maple neck with maple fingerboard (rosewood fingerboard or fretted maple neck from c1969); truss-rod adjuster at body end; one string-guide.
▮ Semi-solid slab single-cutaway body with f-hole; sunburst, naturals or colours.
▮ One plain metal-cover pickup (at neck) and one angled black six-polepiece pickup (in bridgeplate).
▮ Two controls (volume, tone) and three-way selector, all on scratchplate; side-mounted jack socket.
▮ 12-screw pearl laminated plastic scratchplate.
▮ Three-saddle bridge with through-body stringing.

THINLINE TELECASTER second version *1971-79 F-hole body, two humbuckers.*

Body shape 1

Similar to THINLINE TELECASTER first version, except:
▮ Fretted maple neck only; 'bullet' adjuster at headstock.
▮ Three-screw neckplate.
▮ Two metal-cover six-polepiece humbucker pickups.

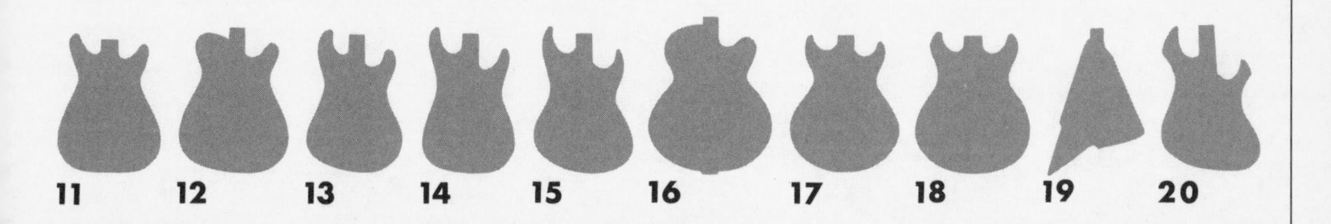

▮ 12-screw pearl, black or white laminated plastic re-styled scratchplate.
▮ Six-saddle small bridge with through-body stringing.

VINTAGE TELECASTER *1982-84 and 1986-current Re-issue based on 1952-period original (see TELECASTER listing in earlier 'Standard' Telecasters section).*

40th ANNIVERSARY TELECASTER *1988-90 Gold hardware, cream scratchplate.*

Body shape 1

Similar to TELECASTER American Standard (see listing in earlier 'Standard' Telecasters section) except:
▮ Fretted maple neck only; pearl tuner buttons.
▮ Bound body with flame maple top; sunburst, natural, or see-through red.
▮ Cream 'grained ivoroid' plastic scratchplate.
▮ Gold-plated hardware.
Custom Shop numbered production run of 300.

FENDER – JAPAN

D'AQUISTO STANDARD *1984 Archtop body with wooden tailpiece, two pickups.*

Body shape 16

▮ Maple glued-in neck with bound rosewood fingerboard; 24.75in scale, 20 frets; truss-rod adjuster at headstock end; pearl tuner buttons; three-tuners-per-side headstock.
▮ Hollow archtop bound single-cutaway body with f-holes; natural, sunburst or black.
▮ Two black 12-polepiece humbucker pickups.
▮ Four controls (two volume, two tones) and three-way selector, all on body; side-mounted jack socket.
▮ Bound floating wooden pickguard.
▮ Single-saddle wooden bridge and tailpiece.

D'AQUISTO ELITE *1984, 1989-current Archtop body with wooden tailpiece, block markers, one pickup.*

Body shape 16

As D'AQUISTO STANDARD, except:
▮ Bound ebony fingerboard; block markers; ebony tuner buttons.
▮ One pickup, type as Standard (metal-cover six-polepiece humbucker on 1989 version).
▮ Two controls (volume, tone) on body.
▮ Gold-plated hardware.

ESPRIT (Standard, Elite or Ultra) *1984 Symmetrical cutaways, three-tuners-per-side headstock, two humbuckers.*

Body shape 18

▮ Maple glued-in neck with rosewood fingerboard (ebony on Ultra), dot markers (blocks on Ultra); 24.75in scale, 22 frets; truss-rod adjuster at headstock end; metal (Standard), pearl (Elite) or ebony (Ultra) tuner buttons; three-tuners-per-side headstock; neck back matches body colour.
▮ Semi-solid carved-top symmetrical cutaways bound body; sunburst or colours.
▮ Two black 12-polepiece humbucker pickups.
▮ Four controls (two volume, two tone) and three-way selector (plus coil-tap, Elite and Ultra), all on body; side-mounted jack socket.
▮ Six-saddle bridge, separate tailpiece.
▮ Gold-plated hardware on Ultra.

ESQUIRE *1986-current Re-issue based on 1950s USA original (see ESQUIRE listing in earlier USA group). Also CUSTOM ESQUIRE, re-issue based on 1960s USA original (see ESQUIRE listing in earlier USA group), sunburst or red.*

FLAME (Standard, Elite or Ultra) *1984 Offset cutaways, three-tuners-per-side headstock, two humbuckers.*

Body shape 17

As ESPRIT (see earlier listing), except:
▮ Smaller body with offset-cutaways.

JAGUAR *1986-current Re-issue based on early 1960s USA original (see JAGUAR listing in earlier USA group); sunburst or colours.*

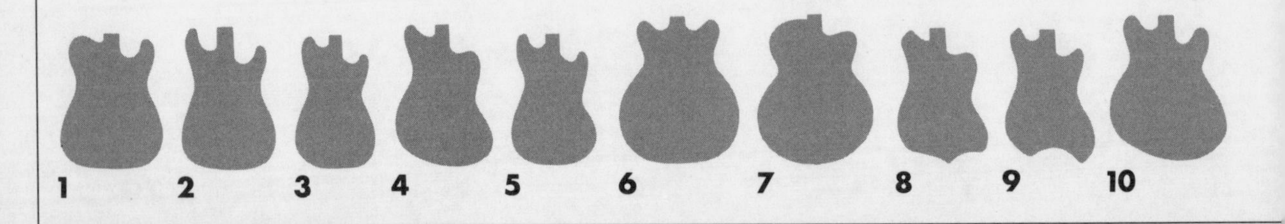

HEARTFIELD

This brandname was used for a range of instruments started in 1989 and built by Fuji, the guitar-makers responsible for Fender Japan production. As part of a reciprocal arrangement, Heartfield is distributed through Fender Musical Instruments USA. The range, designed by both Fender USA and Fender Japan, comprises models considered too radical to appear under the Fender brand, although some do have 'Heartfield By Fender' on the headstock.

JAZZMASTER *1986-current Re-issue based on early 1960s USA original (see JAZZMASTER listing in earlier USA group); sunburst or colours.*

KATANA *1985-86 Triangular 'wedge'-shaped body, 22 frets.*

Body shape 19

- Maple glued-in neck with rosewood fingerboard, triangular markers; 24.75in scale, 22 frets; truss-rod adjuster at headstock end; string clamp; angled headstock and neck matches body colour.
- Bevelled-edge body; various colours.
- Two black coverless humbucker pickups.
- Two controls (volume, tone) and three-way selector, all on body; side-mounted jack socket.
- Re-designed six-saddle bridge/ vibrato unit.

MASTER SERIES *See earlier listings for D'AQUISTO, ESPRIT and FLAME.*

MUSTANG *1986-current Re-issue based on 24in-scale USA original (see MUSTANG listing in earlier USA group).*

PERFORMER *1985-86 Two angled white plain-top pickups.*

Body shape 20

- Maple neck with rosewood fingerboard; 24 frets; truss-rod adjuster at headstock end; string clamp.
- Body sunburst or colours.
- Two angled white plain-top humbucker pickups.
- Two controls (volume, tone), three-way selector and coil-tap, all on scratchplate; side-mounted jack socket.
- 10-screw white laminated plastic scratchplate.
- Re-designed six-saddle bridge/ vibrato unit.

ROBBEN FORD *1989-current Signature on truss-rod cover.*

Body shape 18

Similar to ESPRIT ULTRA (see earlier listing), except:
- Robben Ford signature on truss-rod cover.
- Body sunburst, natural or black.
- Two black coverless humbucker pickups.

STEVENS

Michael Stevens was one of the original guitar-makers hired to run Fender's Custom Shop. Fender Japan began in 1989 to produce some of Stevens' Gibson-influenced designs under the Stevens brandname, but these stopped when Michael left Fender in 1990.

Stratocasters – A-Z listing

CONTEMPORARY STRATOCASTER (six models) *1985-87 22 frets, black headstock, side-mounted jack socket.*

Body shape 2

- Maple neck with rosewood fingerboard; 22 frets; truss-rod adjuster at headstock end; two string-guides (on three higher-priced models); locking nut (string clamp on three lower-priced models); black headstock face; black neck (on three lower-priced models).
- Body various colours.

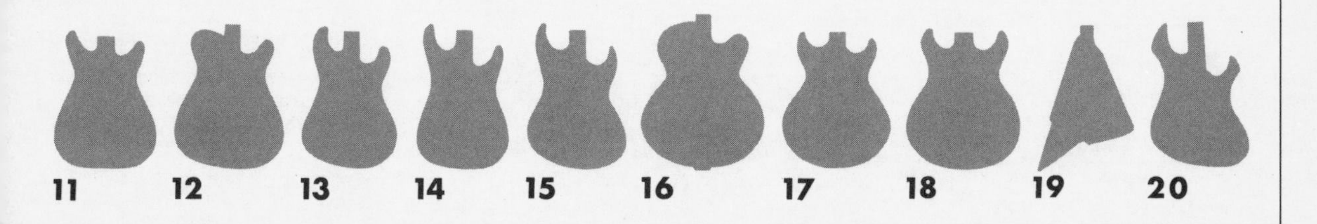

- Black single-coil six-polepiece pickup and/or black coverless humbucker pickup in three layouts: (1) one humbucker; (2) two humbuckers; (3) two single-coils, one humbucker.
- Control layouts: (1) one volume; (2) two controls (volume, tone), three-way selector; plus coil-tap on Deluxe model; (3) two controls (volume, tone), five-way selector, coil-tap; side-mounted jack socket.
- 11-screw black plastic scratchplate (not on one-humbucker model).
- Re-designed six-saddle bridge/vibrato units.
- Black-plated hardware (on three lower-priced models).

HM STRAT first version (two models) *1988-89 Black headstock with large flamboyant "Strat" logo.*

Body shape 14

- Fretted maple neck, or maple neck with rosewood fingerboard; 25in scale, 24 frets; truss-rod adjuster at headstock end; flamboyant "Strat" logo; locking nut; black-faced headstock.
- Smaller body; various colours.
- Black six-polepiece single-coil pickup and/or black coverless humbucker in two layouts: (1) one humbucker, (2) two single-coils, one humbucker.
- Control layouts: (1) volume, tone, coil-tap; (2) volume, two tones, five-way selector, coil-tap; side-mounted jack socket.
- No scratchplate.

- Six-saddle locking bridge/vibrato unit.
- Black-plated hardware.

HM STRAT second version *1991-current Black headstock with small 'stencilled' "Strat" logo.*

Body shape 14

Similar to first version, except:
- 'Stencilled' Strat model logo; single-bar string-guide.
- One single-coil, two humbuckers only.
- Two controls (volume, tone) and five-way selector.

HM STRAT third version *1991-current Droopy headstock with large flamboyant "Fender" logo.*

Body shape 14

- Fretted maple neck, or maple neck with rosewood fingerboard; 25in scale, 22 frets; truss-rod adjuster at headstock end; locking nut; flamboyant "Fender" logo; black-faced headstock; single-bar string-guide.
- Smaller body; various colours.
- Two black coverless humbuckers and one black six-polepiece pickup (in centre).
- Two controls (volume, tone) and five-way selector, all on scratchplate; side-mounted jack socket
- Eight-screw black laminated plastic scratchplate.
- Six-saddle locking bridge/vibrato unit.
- Black-plated hardware.

HRR STRATOCASTER *1990-current 22 frets, Floyd Rose vibrato, bridge humbucker in rectangular cut-out in scratchplate.*

Body shape 2

- Fretted maple neck, or maple neck with rosewood fingerboard; 22 frets; truss-rod adjuster at headstock end; single-bar string-guide; locking nut.
- Body sunburst or colours.
- Two white six-polepiece pickups and one coverless humbucker at bridge.
- Three controls (volume, two tones) and five-way selector, all on scratchplate; jack socket in body face.
- 11-screw white or white-laminated plastic scratchplate.
- Six-saddle locking bridge/vibrato unit.

SHORT SCALE STRATOCASTER *1989-current Two controls, 22 frets.*

Body shape 2

- Fretted maple neck, or maple neck with rosewood fingerboard; 24in scale, 22 frets; truss-rod adjuster at headstock end; one string-guide.
- Body sunburst or colours.
- Three white six-polepiece pickups (pickup at bridge is angled).
- Two controls (volume, tone) and five-way selector, all on scratchplate; jack socket in body face.
- Eight-screw white laminated plastic scratchplate.
- Re-designed six-saddle bridge/vibrato unit.

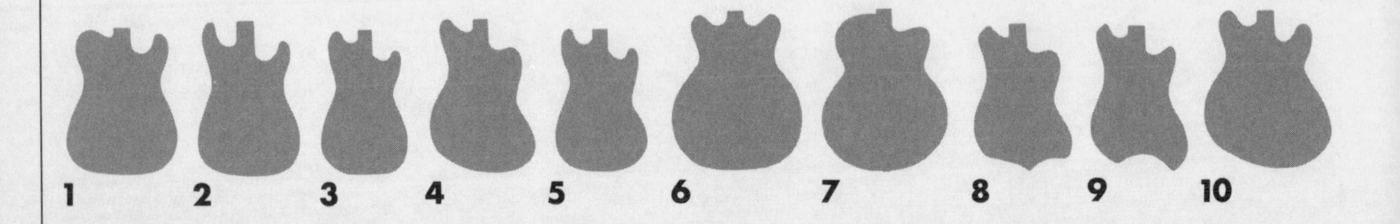

STANDARD '21' (USA)/SPECIAL (UK) *1988-91 Based on Vintage Stratocaster (ie 21 frets – see later 'Vintage' listing), but with two string-guides. These models formerly marketed under the Squier brand. Production moved to Mexico from 1991 (see box in later 'Made in Other Countries' group).*

STANDARD '22' *1985-89 Based on Vintage Stratocaster (see later 'Vintage' listing) but with 22 frets, string clamp and re-designed six-saddle bridge/vibrato unit (locking type from 1988).*

STRAT XII *1988-current 12-string.*

Body shape 2

- Maple neck with rosewood fingerboard; 24.75in scale, 22 frets; truss-rod adjuster at body end; one 'bracket' string-guide.
- Body sunburst only.
- Three white six-polepiece pickups (pickup at bridge is angled).
- Three controls (volume, two tones) and five-way selector, all on scratchplate; jack socket in body face.
- 11-screw white laminated plastic scratchplate.
- 12-saddle bridge with through-body stringing.

VINTAGE STRATOCASTER *1982-current Three models, '57 and '62 ('57 with or without vibrato), based on 1950s and 1960s USA originals (see STRATOCASTER 'pre-CBS' listing in earlier USA group).*

'68 STRATOCASTER *1988-current Re-issue based on late 1960s USA original (see STRATOCASTER 'CBS Sixties' listing in earlier USA group).*

'72 STRATOCASTER *1986-current Re-issue based on early 1970s USA original (see STRATOCASTER 'CBS Seventies' listing in earlier USA group). Also special finish versions: Paisley Red and Blue Flower patterns (1988-current).*

YNGWIE MALMSTEEN STANDARD STRATOCASTER *1991-current Black pickup covers and knobs, signature on headstock.*

Body shape 2

- Scalloped, fretted maple neck; 'bullet' truss-rod adjuster at headstock end; two string-guides; three-screw neckplate.
- Body black, white or blue.
- Three black six-polepiece pickups (pickup at bridge is angled).
- Three controls (volume, two tones) and five-way selector, all on scratchplate; jack socket in body face.
- 11-screw white laminated plastic scratchplate.
- Six-saddle bridge/vibrato unit.

Telecasters – A-Z listing

CONTEMPORARY TELECASTER (two models) *1985-87 Black neck.*

Body shape 1

- Maple neck with rosewood fingerboard; 22 frets; truss-rod adjuster at headstock end; string clamp; black neck back and headstock.
- Slab single-cutaway body; various colours.
- Black six-polepiece single-coil pickup and/or black 12-polepiece humbucker pickup in two layouts: (1) two humbuckers; (2) two single-coils, one humbucker.
- Control layouts: (1) Two controls (volume, tone), three-way selector, coil-tap; (2) Two controls (volume, tone), three mini-toggles; side-mounted jack socket.
- No scratchplate.
- Re-designed six-saddle bridge/vibrato unit.
- Black-plated hardware.

HMT (two models) *1991-current Angled pickup at neck.*

Body shape 1

- Maple neck with rosewood fingerboard, split triangle markers; 25.1in scale, 22 frets; truss-rod adjuster at headstock end; (1) angled droopy pointed headstock, locking nut, or (2) Stratocaster-style headstock.
- Enlarged semi-solid slab single-cutaway body with f-hole; sunburst, natural or colours.

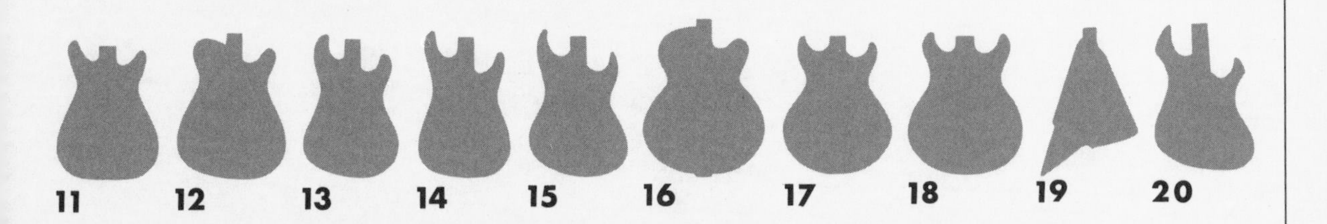

- One angled black plain-top Lace Sensor pickup (at neck) and one black coverless humbucker (at bridge).
- Two controls (volume, tone), three-way selector and coil-tap, all on body; side-mounted jack socket.
- No scratchplate.
- (1) Six-saddle locking bridge/vibrato, or (2) six-saddle small bridge with through-body stringing.

HMT Acoustic-Electric *1991-current Wooden bridge base.*

Body shape 1

- Maple neck with rosewood fingerboard; 25.1in scale, 22 frets; truss-rod adjuster at headstock end; one string-guide.
- Enlarged semi-solid slab single-cutaway body with f-hole; sunburst, natural or colours.
- One angled black plain-top Lace Sensor (at neck) and piezo pickup (in bridge).
- Three controls (volume, pan, tone) on body; side-mounted jack socket.
- No scratchplate.
- Single-saddle wooden-base bridge.

JD TELECASTER *1992-current Black six-polepiece pickup at neck.*

Body shape 1

Based on 1992 Jerry Donahue USA Custom Shop original. As Japanese '62' CUSTOM TELECASTER (see later listing), except:
- Fretted maple neck.
- Black six-polepiece pickup (at neck).
- Five-way selector.
- Eight-screw black laminated plastic scratchplate.

STANDARD (USA)/SPECIAL (UK) *1988-91 Based on normal Telecaster style, but fretted maple neck only, six-saddle bridge/tailpiece, no through-body stringing; blond or black finish only, white scratchplate. These models marketed under the Squier brand c1985-88. Production moved to Mexico from 1991.*

'52 TELECASTER *1982-current Re-issue based on early 1950s USA original (see TELECASTER listing in earlier USA group). Marketed under Squier brand outside Japan until c1985; reintroduced under Fender brand in USA and UK from c1990.*

'62 CUSTOM TELECASTER *1985-current Re-issue based on 1960s USA bound original (see TELECASTER listing in earlier USA group); sunburst or red.*

'69 BLUE FLOWER TELECASTER *1986-current Re-issue based on late 1960s patterned-finish USA original (see TELECASTER listing in earlier USA group).*

'69 PAISLEY RED TELECASTER *1986-current Re-issue based on late 1960s patterned-finish USA original (see TELECASTER listing in earlier USA group).*

'69 ROSEWOOD TELECASTER *1986-current Re-issue based on USA original (see listing in earlier USA group).*

'69 THINLINE TELECASTER *1986-current Re-issue based on earlier USA single-coil-equipped original (see first version listing in earlier USA group); natural only.*

'72 TELECASTER CUSTOM *1986-current Re-issue based on 1970s USA original with humbucker (see listing in earlier USA group); sunburst or black.*

'72 THINLINE TELECASTER *1986-current Re-issue based on later USA twin-humbucker-equipped original (see second version listing in earlier USA group); natural only.*

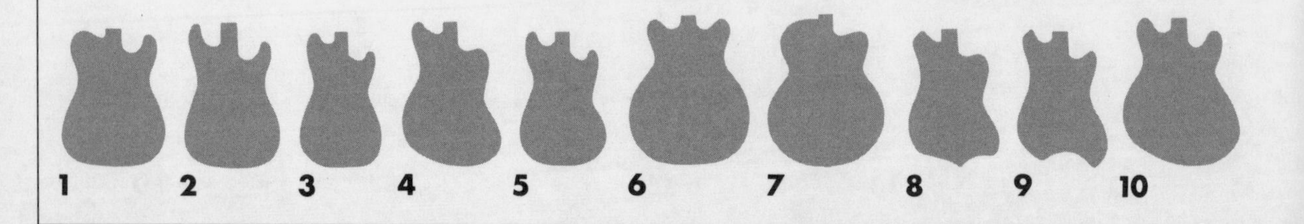

SQUIER – JAPAN

BULLET H2 *1983-84*

Body shape 13

As Fender USA version (see listing in earlier USA group), except:
- Body black or sunburst.
- Re-designed six-saddle bridge/tailpiece with no through-body stringing.

BULLET S3 *1983-84*

Body shape 13

As Fender USA version (see listing in earlier USA group), except:
- Body black or sunburst.
- Re-designed six-saddle bridge/tailpiece with no through-body stringing.
- Bridge/vibrato unit option.

BULLET S3T *1985-88*

Body shape 13

As BULLET S3, except:
- Maple neck with rosewood fingerboard; truss-rod adjuster at headstock end; Stratocaster-style headstock.
- Body black or red.
- Three white six-polepiece pickups (pickup at bridge is angled).
- Re-designed six-saddle bridge/vibrato unit.

CONTEMPORARY BULLET HST *1985-88 No scratchplate.*

Body shape 13

- Maple neck with rosewood fingerboard; truss-rod adjuster at headstock end; 'star' bullet logo; one string-guide; Stratocaster style headstock.
- Body black or white.
- Two black six-polepiece pickups and one black coverless humbucker pickup (at bridge).
- Two controls (volume, tone) and five-way selector, all on body; side-mounted jack socket.
- No scratchplate.
- Re-designed six-saddle bridge/vibrato unit.

KATANA *1985-86 Triangular 'wedge'-shaped body, 21 frets.*

Body shape 19

- Maple neck with rosewood fingerboard; 24.75in scale, 21 frets; truss-rod adjuster at body end; two string-guides.
- Bevelled-edge body; black or white.
- One black coverless humbucker pickup.
- One control (volume) on body; side-mounted jack socket.
- Six-saddle bridge/vibrato unit.

Stratocasters – A-Z listing

CONTEMPORARY (three models) *1985-87 Black headstock.*

Body shape 2

- Maple neck with rosewood fingerboard; 25.5in scale (24.75in on early versions), 22 frets (21 on one-humbucker model); truss-rod adjuster at headstock end (body end on one-humbucker model); two string-guides; black headstock face (and black neck on early versions).
- Body various colours.
- Black six-polepiece single-coil pickup and/or black coverless humbucker pickup in three layouts: (1) one humbucker; (2) two humbuckers; (3) two single-coils, one humbucker.
- Control layouts: (1) one volume; (2) two controls (volume, tone), three-way selector; (3) two controls (volume, tone), three mini-toggles; side-mounted jack socket (not on one-humbucker model).
- No scratchplate.
- Six-saddle bridge/vibrato unit.

HANK MARVIN *1992-current Limited edition based on 1950s USA model (see STRATOCASTER 'pre-CBS' listing in earlier USA group); red only; Hank Marvin signature on headstock.*

POPULAR (UK)/'70s (USA) *1983-85 Based on mid-1970s USA original (see STRATOCASTER 'CBS Seventies' listing*

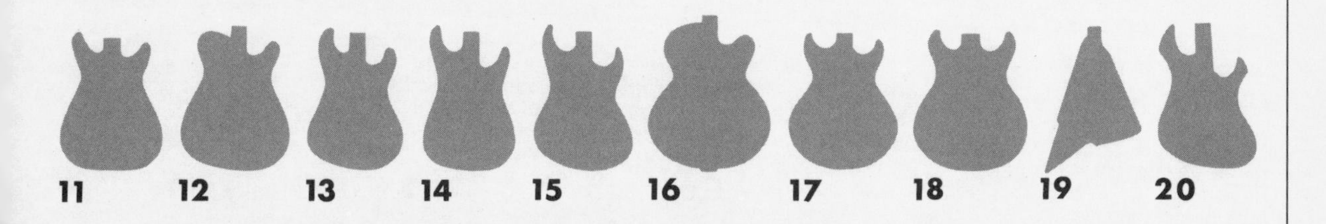

in earlier USA group); replaced by version with Fender Japan brandname in 1985. The first Squier electric to be made available in the USA.

SILVER SERIES *1992-current As STANDARD (85-88), but "Silver Series" on headstock.*

STANDARD 1985-88 *Based on 1950s and 1960s USA originals (see STRATOCASTER 'pre-CBS' listing in earlier USA group); two string-guides. Replaced by version with Fender Japan brandname in 1988. Also models with locking nut and re-designed six-saddle bridge/vibrato unit (1987-88).*

VINTAGE *1982-85 Two models, '57 and '62, based on 1950s and 1960s USA originals (see STRATOCASTER 'pre-CBS' listing in earlier USA group). Early examples have small Squier logo and large Fender brandname on headstock; later examples have small Fender logo and large Squier brandname.*

Telecasters – A-Z listing

POPULAR (UK)/'70s (USA) *1983-85 Based on mid 1970s original (see TELECASTER listing in earlier USA group); fretted maple neck only; blond or black, with white or black laminated plastic scratchplate respectively.*

SILVER SERIES *1992-current As 'STANDARD' (85-88), but "Silver Series" on headstock.*

STANDARD *1985-88 Based on 1983-84 USA original (see STANDARD TELECASTER listing in earlier USA group); fretted maple neck only; body blond or black. Replaced by version with Fender Japan brandname in 1988.*

VINTAGE *1982-85 Based on 1950s USA originals (see TELECASTER listing in earlier USA group); black or white plastic scratchplate. Early examples have small Squier logo and large Fender brandname on headstock; later examples have small Fender logo and large Squier brandname.*

OTHER COUNTRIES

INDIA

As part of a constant re-assessment of production costs and sourcing, Fender USA contracted for instruments to be made at a guitar factory in India during 1989 and 1990. These Strat-style models appeared as Squier II Stratocasters in America and as Sunn Mustangs in other countries.

KOREA

Although Fender's Bullet models of the early 1980s originally used Korean-made bodies and necks, the company did not begin full production in Korea until 1985. Since then various Stratocaster- and Telecaster-based models have been produced, including Standard, Contemporary, HM and FR series, all under the Squier brandname.

MEXICO

Fender's Mexican facility was established in 1990. Production of the Fender Standard Stratocaster and Telecaster was transferred from Japan to Mexico in 1991.

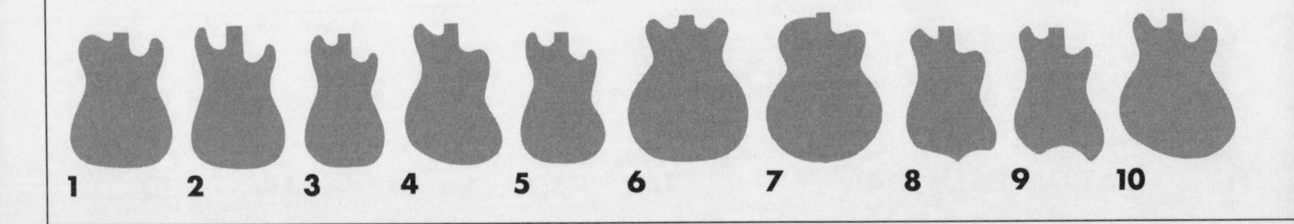

DATING FENDER GUITARS

Finding a method to date a guitar is important. Not only can it help satisfy an owner's natural curiosity about the origins of an instrument but, in the case of desirable instruments, the vintage can have a great bearing on the guitar's value. The Fender brand has its fair share of collectibles, of course, and as prices of the more sought-after models often reach very high levels any corroboratory clues that indicate the year of production assume increased importance.

However, as with the guitars of virtually all manufacturers, no dating of Fenders should be taken as gospel. It is impossible to pinpoint exactly the precise occasions when production changes were made. In all instances there would be transition periods when old components would be used up, sometimes combined with new parts and construction methods. Fender instruments have used certain dated items and as long as these and the various general and specific changes tally to within one or two years, then the instrument can be attributed to that period.

Fender's erstwhile factory manager Forrest White has warned us against the dangers of placing too much importance on what he describes as "Fender fiction" (see page 48), in other words the attempts to date exactly the results of a mass-production assembly line which did not necessarily use dated components in a strict chronological fashion. To allot exact dates within such a manufacturing process is almost impossible, and doing so can be both risky and misleading. It is a pity that nowadays so much emphasis is placed on the so-called 'exact' age of a Fender guitar; often the vintage assumes more importance and more relevance to value than the actual quality of the particular instrument.

Changes specific to each Fender have been indicated in the preceding instrument listing. Although the respective features on some individual models can provide more dating clues than others, there are comparatively few aspects that are consistent across the Fender range, and fewer still that have chronological significance. Such relevant general pointers to production dates of USA-made models are shown here, but even these must not be regarded as infallible because it is known that the components in question were not always used in any strict sequence.

NECKPLATE

The standard Fender method of fixing the neck to the body is via four screws, and this is accomplished using a re-inforcing metal neckplate. The rectangular four-screw type has been used since the inception of Fender's first solid electric, providing a simple and secure foundation for the neck.

From 1971 to 1981 a restyled, three-screw version (actually two screws and one bolt) was used on certain models only, namely: Stratocaster; Telecaster Custom, Deluxe and Thinline; and Starcaster. After 1981 Fender reverted to the four-screw type for all instruments (excluding the glued-neck models, of course).

From 1954 to 1976 the neckplate carried a stamped serial number. From 1976 onward the number appears on the headstock face, except for the Vintage re-issues and limited editions.

From 1965 to 1983 the neckplate (both four- and three-screw types) was stamped with a large, reversed 'F'.

MACHINE HEADS

It was not initially easy for Fender to find suitable machine heads for Leo's ideal of a small, neat headstock with straight string-pull. This problem was solved by using products supplied by the Chicago-based Kluson company, although even these had to be cut down by Race & Olmsted to squeeze them into the minimal length decreed by the headstock design. The Klusons used by Fender each had a 'safety string post', a slotted shaft with a central vertical hole designed to take the end of the string and thus eliminate the unsightly and dangerous protruding string length. These machine heads were used from 1950 to c1966, and the variations of the markings on their metal covers can provide an indication of date.

Version 1, used in 1950 and 1951, has 'Kluson Deluxe' and 'Pat. Appld' stamped on the cover.

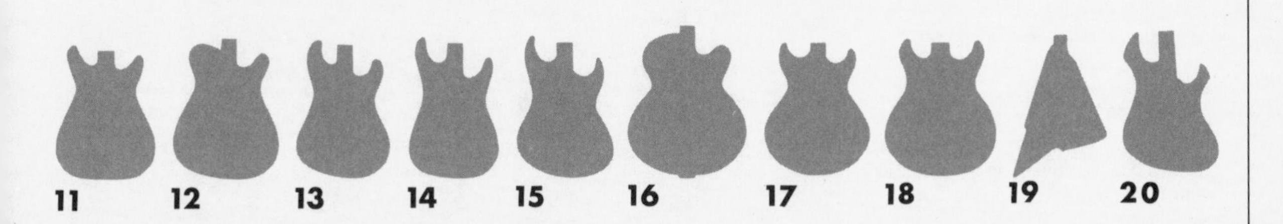

Version 2, used from 1951 to c1955, has no markings on the cover.

Version 3, used from c1955 to c1964, has 'Kluson Deluxe' stamped in a single, central, vertical line on the cover.

Version 4, used from c1964 to c1966, has 'Kluson' and 'Deluxe' stamped in two parallel, vertical lines on the cover.

Due to supply and quality problems with Kluson, Leo Fender wanted a machine head produced in-house, and in 1965 contracted Race & Olmsted to supply a revised, cheaper design. The result was a machine head with an angled baseplate, 'F'-stamped cover, and a less rounded button. It was used on Fender instruments until c1976 when it was replaced by a more competitively-priced version made by the German Schaller company, which was fitted until c1983. Although ostensibly very similar in appearance, the Schaller unit has a different construction, and can be distinguished by its closed cover, with no visible axle-end on the side.

NECK/FINGERBOARD CONSTRUCTION

From 1950 to 1959 Fender used a one-piece, fretted, maple neck, with no separate fingerboard.

From 1959 to 1962 the top of the maple neck was planed flat and fitted with a rosewood fingerboard, flat on the base and cambered on the top. The appearance when viewed from the body end of the neck provides its 'slab-board' description.

From 1962 to 1983 the top of the maple neck was cambered and fitted with a thin-section rosewood fingerboard which followed the same curve. Again, the neck-end appearance provides its 'veneer' description. A maple fingerboard was offered as an option, officially from 1967 but often supplied prior to this date. In 1969 the one-piece fretted maple neck was reinstated as an alternative to the rosewood fingerboard. (See opposite page, top left, for 'slab' and 'veneer' examples.)

Since 1983 Fender have reverted to a 'slab' rosewood fingerboard, while still offering the option of their one-piece, fretted, maple neck.

NECK DATES

For production purposes, Fender provided dates on various components, one of the most consistent and obvious being the neck. The date is to be found on the body-end, either pencilled or rubber-stamped. There have been times when the neck didn't carry this useful information, the longest period being between 1973 and 1981, and for these instruments other dating clues have to suffice.

SERIAL NUMBERS

These should be regarded as merely a guide to dating, with the apparent production year being confirmed by other aspects of each instrument. Fender serial numbers were not assigned in exact chronological order, nor were neckplates used on a strict rotational basis, so apparent discrepancies of even several years can occur. Numbers can be located on either the bridgeplate, backplate, neckplate, or headstock.

USA number series	Circa	
Up to 6000	1950-54	
Up to 10,000	1954-56	4 or 5 digits (inc 0 or – prefix)
10,000s	1955-56	4 or 5 digits (inc 0 or – prefix)
10,000s to 20,000s	1957	5 or 6 digits (inc 0 or – prefix)
20,000s to 30,000s	1958	5 or 6 digits (inc 0 or – prefix)
30,000s to 40,000s	1959	
40,000s to 50,000s	1960	
50,000s to 70,000s	1961	
60,000s to 90,000s	1962	
80,000s to 90,000s	1963	
Up to L10,000	1963	L + 5 digits
L10,000s to L20,000s	1963	L + 5 digits
L20,000s to L50,000s	1964	L + 5 digits
L50,000s to L90,000s	1965	L + 5 digits
100,000s	1965	
100,000s to 200,000s	1966-67	
200,000s	1968	
200,000s to 300,000s	1969-70	
300,000s	1971-72	
300,000s to 500,000s	1973	
400,000s to 500,000s	1974-75	
500,000s to 700,000s	1976	
76 or S6 + 5 digits	1976	
S7 or S8 + 5 digits	1977	
S7, S8 or S9 + 5 digits	1978	
S9 or E0 + 5 digits	1979	
S9, E0 or E1 + 5 digits	1980-81	
E1, E2 or E3 + 5 digits	1982	
E2 or E3 + 5 digits	1983	
E3 or E4 + 5 digits	1984-85	
E4 + 5 digits	1987	
E4 or E8 + 5 digits	1988	
E8 or E9 + 5 digits	1989-	
E9 or N9 + 5 digits	1990-	
N0 + 5 digits	1990-	
N1 + 5/6 digits	1991-	
N2 + 5/6 digits	1992-	

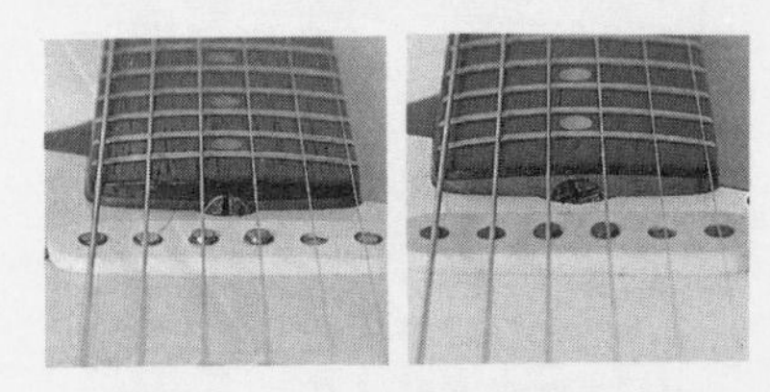

Slab/veneer fingerboards (above). The 'slab' fingerboard (left) has a straight join between neck and fingerboard, while the 'veneer' fingerboard (right) reveals a curved join.

Headstocks (below). Headstock shape is only of use to date Fenders in the case of the Stratocaster. The most obvious change from the original (left, 1954-65) was to the enlarged version (centre, 1965-82). After 1982 Fender reverted to smaller versions (example, right) based on the original.

These numbers (opposite) represent the bulk of Fender's American production. There are various anomalies, odd series, special prefixes and the like, but as these have no overall dating relevance they are not shown. Also excluded are the series used on Vintage re-issues, limited editions and so on; these are specific to certain models and not pertinent to age.

The listing shown on page 92 does not apply to any non-USA manufactured Fenders; these have their own various number series, which unfortunately do sometimes duplicate the American system. Any confusion has to be resolved by studying other aspects of the instruments to determine correct origins and production dates.

Fender Japan production commenced in 1982 and the company have used a series of prefixes to indicate the year of manufacture. However, this is approximate and, again, should be used as a general guide only.

Japan number series	Circa
JV + 5 digits	1982-84
SQ + 5 digits	1983-84
E + 6 digits	1984-87
A + 6 digits	1985-86
B + 6 digits	1985-86
C + 6 digits	1985-86
F + 6 digits	1986-87
G + 6 digits	1987-88
H + 6 digits	1988-89
I + 6 digits	1989-90
J + 6 digits	1989-90
K + 6 digits	1990-91
L + 6 digits	1991-92
M + 6 digits	1992-current

Fender Japan have confirmed evidence that certain series have been used beyond the production spans listed above, in particular the A-, C- and G-prefixed numbers. This underlines the need for caution when dating by using serial numbers.

PART NUMBERS

Many Fender catalogues and pricelists of relatively recent years have included 'part numbers' for each model. For instance, the complete part number for a current Fender Stratocaster American Standard might read 010-7400-775. The digits indicate a number of factors including hardware options, country of origin, model number, maple or rosewood fingerboard, if the guitar comes with or without case, and its colour. Of most use are the second and third numbers, which indicate country of origin (10 in our example).

- 10 USA
- 13 Formerly Japan, now Mexico/USA
- 14 USA/Mexico
- 25 Japan
- 26 Japan (Squier)
- 27 Formerly Korea (few), now Japan
- 28 Formerly Japan, then India (Squier II, Sunn)
- 29 India (Squier II, Sunn)
- 31 Japan (Heartfield)
- 32 Japan (Squier, since 1992)
- 33 Korea (Squier)

Page numbers in **bold** refer to illustrations, and in *italics* to reference listings.

Acuff, Roy 9
Alex Gregory model 59
anodised scratchplate **18**, 24
antigua finish 37, *76, 80, 83*
Aria 49
'Arrow' *70, 80*
Australia 29

Baldwin 32
Barden, Joe 57
Bates, Art 17
Beatles, The 29, 36, 40-41
Beck, Jeff 50, 55, 57, *78*
Beers, Ronnie **7**
Bigsby, Paul 13
his guitar compared to Fender 13, 21
Blanda, George 56, 57
'block' fingerboard markers 37
blond finish 13, 25
Blue flower *see* Stratocaster/Telecaster
bound body 28
bound fingerboard 37
brass hardware 44
Britain 29
Broadcaster model **11**, 13, 16, *70*
Bigsby comparison 13
and Gretsch 16
name changed to Telecaster 16
Broadkaster (Gretsch drum) **11**, 16
Bronco model **31**, 40, 41, *70*
Bryant, Jimmy 16-17
bullet truss-rod adjuster 39
Bullet models 44, *70-71, 89*
Burton, James **47**, 55, 57, *82*
Byrds, The 36

Canada 29
Carruthers, John 56
Carson, Bill
and Stratocaster 20-21, *72*
CBS *see* Columbia Broadcasting System
Charvel 61
chronology of all models 68-69
Clapton, Eric 25, **47**, 54, 55,.57, *77*
Cole, Mike 17
Collector's Series 43
'Collectibles' series 60
Collins, Albert 57, *81*
colour chart **23**
Columbia Broadcasting System
build new Fender factory 37
factory improvements 48
income during 1970s 44
Korean manufacturing 44
Missile Way factory 37
production halted 1980s 45
profit motive 32-33
purchase of Fender companies 29-32
quality of Fender products 33, 41
recruit ex-Yamaha management 44-45
sell Fender 52
Squier name acquired 49, 63
and 'spare-parts' guitars 40
Contemporary Bullet model *89*
Cooley, Spade **10**
Coronado models **30**, 37, *71*
antigua finish 37, *71*
Wildwood finish 37, *71*
Cort 53
country-of-origin codes 93
Cray, Robert 57, *78*
Cropper, Steve **47**
custom colours **22-23**, 25-26
Custom model **34**, 40, *72*
Custom Esquire model *see* Esquire
Custom Shop 56-60, **58-59**, *72*
Custom Telecaster model *see* Telecaster
Czechoslovakia 61

D'Aquisto models 52, *84*
dating Fenders 66, 91-93
DeArmond 30
Donahue, Jerry 57, *82*
Douglas, Jon *78*
Driver, Dave 17
Ducco finishes 25
Duo-Sonic model **19**, 24, 41, *72*
DuPont paints 23, 25, 26

Electric XII model **26**, 34, 36, 40, *72*
Epiphone 12, 13
Epstein, Brian 41
Esprit models 52, **63,** *84*
Esquire model **11**, 13, 41, *72, 84*
early versions 13
Custom 28, *73*
1960 re-issue *72*

Fender, Esther 13
Fender Electric Instrument Co 9
exports 29
financial problems 13, 20
logo change 28-29
new buildings at South Pomona 9
new buildings at South Raymond 17
plan first electric solid 12
sale to CBS 29-32
success in early 1960s 29
Fender Japan **62-63**
business arrangement 45
established 45
first non-Japan-market models 52
individual models *see* under model name
major Fender producer mid-1980s 53
original models Japan only 49
tenth anniversary guitar **62**
Vintage re-issue production 48
Fender, Leo **7**
and business aims post-war 12
on CBS 36
as consultant to CBS 36
dies 1991 36, 50
didn't play guitar 24
early years 8
eye disability 9
forms Fender Electric Instrument Co 9
and G&L 36
and K&F 9
leaves CBS 36
and Music Man 36
and Stratocaster design 20
virus complaints 32
virus cured 36
Fender Musical Instruments Corp
Brea HQ 52
Corona factory 53
Mexican factory 61
production halted 1985 52
purchase company from CBS 52
Scottsdale HQ 52
search for new factory 52
Fender, Phyllis 5
Fender Radio Service 8
Fender-Rhodes piano 41
Fender Sales Inc
formation 17
sale to CBS 29-32
Fernandes 49
Fields, Gene 36-37, 41
Flame models 52, *84*
Ford, Robben *85*
FR models *90*
Freeman
and Marauder design 36
Frost, Al 13
Fuji Gen-Gakki 48, 53, *85*
Fullerton, George **7**, **15**
on CBS 33
and custom colours 26
joins Fender 12
leaves Fender 36
on Jimmy Bryant 16-17

G&L 36
Galleon, Rex 20
Gatton, Danny 57, *81*
'German carve'
technique 31, 40
Germany 29, 61
Gibson 12, 21, 37, 41, 52, 60, 61
Gilmour, David 15
glued-in neck 52, 60
Godin 52
gold-plated hardware 24
Gomez, Tadeo **7**
Greco 48
'green' scratchplate 22
Gregory, Maestro Alex 59
Gretsch **11**, 16, 24, 28, 37
Gruhn, George 25
Gupton, Dave 41, 45
Hall, Francis 9, 17
Hamer 60
hang-tag 19
Harmony *75*
Harrison, George 41
Hayes, Charlie 17
Haynes, Homer 14, 57, 59, *77*
Heartfield *85*
Hendrix, Jimi 40, **47**, *76*
'hockey-stick' headstock 36, 37
Holly, Buddy **47**
Homer & Jethro 57
Hondo 52
humbucking pickups 35, 39, 41, 47, 60
Hyatt, Dale
on CBS 33
joins Fender 12
leaves Fender 36
as salesman for Fender Sales Inc 17
on selling guitars from factory 13
on selling early Stratocasters 21

Ibanez 48, 49, 61
India 61, *90*
international colours 43
International Music Co 52

Jackson 52, 53, 60, 62
Jaguar model **26**, 28-29, 41, 60, *73, 84*
Japan 29, 45, 48-49, 53, 58, 62-63
Japanese copies 45
Jazzmaster model **18**, 24-25, 41, 60, *73, 85*

K&F 9
Kaman Music Corp 52
Kanda Shokai 45
Katana model 53, **63,** *85*
Kauffman, 'Doc' **7**
and K&F 9
meets Leo Fender 8-9
Kawai 48
Kaye, Mary **55**, *78*
Kluson 91-92
Korea 44, 53, *70, 90*

Lace, Don 56
Lace Sensor 50, 56
Lead models **43**, 44, *73*
Lennon, John 41
locking vibrato 60
LTD model **31**, 40, *73-74*
Lugar, Louis **7**

machine heads
as dating clue 91-92
Malmsteen, Yngwie 54, 57, *79*
Marauder model **27**, 36
marble finish *76, 81*
Martin 28, 57
Martin, Fred 28
Marvin, Hank 14, 59, 63, *89*

Master Series 52, 53, *85*
Maverick model **34**, 40, *72, 74*
McCartney, Paul 41
McLaren, John 45
Mexico 50, 61, *75, 87, 90*
Miller, Mudge 41
Montego models **31,** 40, *74*
Moridaira 53
Music Man 36
'Musiclander' *74, 80*
Musicmaster models **19**, 24, 41, *74*
Mustang model **27**, 29, 60, *74-75, 85*
mute (Jaguar) **26**, 28

National 12, 13
neck dates 48, 92
neckplates 48, 91
  with 'F' stamp 29, 91
neck widths 28
Nelson, Rick 55
'No-casters' 16, *70*
Nordoff-Robbins 58

Olmsted, Karl
  meets Leo Fender 12
  see also Race & Olmsted
Ovation 52
Owens, Buck 28

Pacific Music Supply 9
Page, John
  and Bullet design 44
  and Custom Shop 56
  on early Custom Shop runs 57
  joins Fender 44
  and Performer design 53
Paisley red *see* Stratocaster/Telecaster
part numbers 93
Patton, Don 17
Paul, Les 12
Performer model 53, **62**, *85*
Perine, Bob 6
'player's choice' colours 25
'pre-CBS' 32
Presley, Elvis 55
Prodigy models **50**, 61, *75*

Race & Olmsted 91
  early business with Fender 12
  Stratocaster parts 21
Radio & Television Equipment Co 9
  move to Fender Sales Inc 17
Randall, Don **7**
  and Beatles 40-41
  on CBS 33-36
  and custom colours 28
  and early distribution of Fender 9
  and export of Fender products 29
  forms Fender Sales Inc 17
  and increase in Fender sales 29
  leaves Fender 36
  names Fender models 16
  and sale of Fender to CBS 32
  on Stratocaster 20
Regal *75*
Rey, Alvino 25
Rhodesia 29
Rich, Don 28
Richard, Cliff 14
Rickenbacker 8, 12, 36, 37
Robben Ford model *85*
Rose, Floyd **51**, 60, *77, 78, 82*
rosewood fingerboard 25
Rosewood Telecaster model *see* Telecaster
Rossmeisl, Roger 31, 37-40
  and Coronado 37
  and LTD 40
  and Montego 40

Sambora, Richie 60
Scandinavia 29
Schaller 92
Schultz, Bill
  joins Fender 45
  and purchase of Fender 52
  recommends investment package 45
  suggests Japanese production 45
serial numbers 48, 92-93
Shadows, The 14
short scale 29, 62
Simoni, Virgilio 'Babe' 37, 40
'slab' fingerboard 92, **93**
Smith, Dan
  on CBS selling Fender 52
  on Floyd Rose hardware 60
  joins Fender 45
  on headstock trademarks 61
  on licences for Fender Japan 48
  on market requirements 60
  and return to four-bolt Strat 45
  on three-bolt Squier Strat 49
  on Vintage re-issues 48-49
Smith, Richard 13
South Africa 29
Squier
  Bullet models *89*
  Contemporary Stratocaster *89*
  early logo 49, **63**
  first models 49
  Hank Marvin model **63**, *89*
  Katana model *89*
  Korean-made models *90*
  Made In USA models *75*
  Popular Stratocaster *89*
  Popular Telecaster *90*
  Silver Series 63, *90*
  Standard Stratocaster *90*
  Standard Telecaster *90*
  Vintage Stratocaster *90*
  Vintage Telecaster *90*
  70s re-issue Stratocaster 49, *89-90*
Squier, V C 49, 63
Squier II *90*
Starcaster model **38**, 41, *75*
Stevens *85*
Stevens, Michael 56, *85*
Strat model *see* Stratocaster
Strat Plus model *see* Stratocaster
Stratocaster model **14-15**, 20-21, **22**, **23**, **31**, **38**, **39**, *75-76*
  American Standard **51**, 56, *76*
  Bigsby comparison 21
  Bill Carson model *72*
  Blue flower *87*
  Contemporary 53, *79, 85*
  eight-string by Custom Shop 60
  Elite **47**, 49, *76*
  Eric Clapton model **54**, 57, *77*
  Floyd Rose Classic 60, *77*
  Gold/Gold **43,** *77*
  Hank Marvin model **59,** *72*
  headstock enlarged 31, 37
  Hendrix model *76*
  HLE 57, **59**, *77*
  HM Strat *86*
  HM Strat Ultra *77*
  HRR 60, *86*
  Jeff Beck model 57, *78*
  'Mary Kaye' models **55**, *78*
  Paisley red *87*
  Popular 49
  'Rhinestone' *78*
  Robert Cray model 57, *78*
  Set Neck models 60, *78*
  serial number 0001 15
  seven-string prototypes **59**
  Short-scale model **62**, *86*
  Special *87*
  Standard 45, **46**, 49, *87*
  Stevie Ray Vaughan model **55**, 57, *78*
  Strat **43**, 44, *79*
  Strat Plus **50**, 56, *79*
  Strat Walnut **47**, *79*
  Strat XII **62**, *87*
  Texas Special *72*
  three-bolt neck 39
  US Strat Ultra **51**, *79*
  vibrato design 21
  Vintage '57/'62 **46**, 48, *79, 87*
  Yngwie Malmsteen model **54**, 57, *79, 87*
  25th Anniversary model 41, **42**, *80*
  35th Anniversary model 51, *80*
  '68 re-issue *87*
  '72 re-issue *87*
Stuart, Fred **59**
'student' models 24
sunburst finish
  two-tone **15**, 21
  three-tone **23**, 25
Sunn *90*
Swinger model **34**, 40, *80*

Tavares, Freddie **7**
  joins Fender 17
  and Jazzmaster design 24
  and Stratocaster design 20
Telecaster model **10**, 13, 16, **23**, *80-81*
  Albert Collins model 57, *81*
  American Standard **51**, 56, *81*
  Black & Gold **47**, *81*
  Blue flower **35**, 40, 60, *80, 88*
  Contemporary 53, *87*
  Custom (bound) **23**, 28, 80, *88*
  Custom (humbucker) **39**, 41, *83, 88*
  Danny Gatton model 57, **59**, *81*
  Deluxe **39**, 41, *83*
  Elite **47**, 49, *81*
  HMT models *87-88*
  James Burton model **55**, 57, *82*
  JD model *88*
  Jerry Donahue model 57, *82, 88*
  'Knebworth' model **58**
  Paisley **35**, 40, 60, *80, 88*
  Plus *83*
  Rosewood **35**, 41, 60, *82, 88*
  Set Neck models **51**, 60, *82*
  Special *88*
  Standard **46**, 49, *88*
  Texas Special *72*
  Thinline **35**, 40, 41, 60, *83, 88*
  Vintage **47**, 48, *84, 88*
  40th Anniversary model 57, *84*
  '52 re-issue (*see* also Vintage) *88*
Thinline Telecaster model *see Telecaster*
three-quarter size models 24
Tokai 48, 49
trademarks 61
Travis, Merle 13

Vaughan, Stevie Ray 55, 57, *78*
'veneer' fingerboard 92, **93**
Ventures, The **47**
vintage guitars, popularity of 48
Vintage re-issue models 48

Welch, Bruce 14
West, Speedy 16
White, Forrest **7**
  on CBS 32-33
  on dating Fenders 48, 91
  and Jazzmaster circuit 24-25
  joins Fender 20
  leaves Fender 36
  meets Leo Fender 17
  and quality incentive scheme 20
Wildwood finish **30**, 37, *71*
Wilkinson roller nut 56
Wilkinson, Trev 56
Wilson, Gregg 44

Yamaha 44, 49
Yamano Music 45
Young Chang 53
'You won't part with yours either' advertising campaign **6**, **19**, **26**
Yugoslavia 61

Zimbabwe 29

Guitars photographed came from the following individuals' collections, and we are grateful for their help: Robin Baird; Simon Carlton; David Gilmour; Robin Guthrie; Rick Harrison (Music Ground); Paul Midgley; Tom Nolan (Fender A&R London); Tim Philips; Bruce Welch. Our photographers were: Matthew Chattle; Garth Blore; Nigel Bradley & Will Taylor. Thanks also to John Entwistle, Maestro Alex Gregory, Gerry Kelly, Alan Rogan/Mike Doyle and Norma Velvikis (The Phelps Group) for supplying existing photographs.

Memorabilia came from the collections of Tony Bacon, Paul Day, George Fullerton, Don Randall, Alan Rogan, Steve Soest (Soest Guitar Repair), and Arthur Soothill (Tuned Percussion London), all photographed by Tony Bacon (with thanks to Will).

We would also like to thank: Lawrence Acunto (20th Century Guitar); Julie Bowie; Dave Burrluck (Guitar Magazine); Bill Carson & Susan Carson; Doug Chandler (Chandler Guitars); Richard Chapman (Guitar Magazine/ Christie's); Cheryl Clark (G&L); Paul Colbert (Vox); Andy Cooper; Merelyn Davis; Jane, Sarah & Simon Day; André Duchossoir; Phyllis Fender; George Fullerton & Lucille Fullerton; Alan Greenwood (Vintage Guitar); Bob Henrit; Dale Hyatt & Eileen Hyatt; Tom James; Mike Kaskell; Mel Lambert; Jon Lewin (Making Music); Neville Marten (Guitarist); Charles Measures (Guitar Gallery UK); Howard Meek; Karl Olmsted & Katherine Olmsted; Steve Preston (Arbiter); Don Randall; Jim Roberts (Bass Player); Johnny Saitoh & Sam Sekihara (Fender Japan); Dan Smith, John Page, Fred Stuart, Mike Lewis (Fender USA); Richard Smith; Steve Soest & Amy Soest (Soest Guitar Repair); Phil Taylor (David Gilmour Music); Guy Wallace (Music Man); Jim Werner; Forrest White.

Unsourced quotations in the text are taken from original interviews with Phyllis Fender, George Fullerton, Dale Hyatt, Karl Olmsted, John Page, Don Randall, Dan Smith and Forrest White conducted by Tony Bacon in California during February 1992, and from a spoken-to-tape commentary recorded by Bill Carson especially for this project in September 1991. The sources of previously published quotations are given where they occur in the text.

Books consulted during research include: Tony Bacon & Paul Day *The Guru's Guitar Guide* (Track Record 1992), *The Ultimate Guitar Book* (Dorling Kindersley 1991); Donald Brosnac *Guitar History I* (Bold Strummer 1986); André Duchossoir *The Fender Stratocaster* (Mediapresse 1988); *The Fender Telecaster* (Hal Leonard 1991), *Guitar Identification* (Hal Leonard 1990); George Gruhn & Walter Carter *Gruhn's Guide to Vintage Guitars* (GPI 1991); Guitar Magazine (Japan) *The Fender Stratocaster* (Rittor 1987); Tom Wheeler *American Guitars* (Harper Perennial 1990); YMM Player *History of Electric Guitars* (Player Corporation 1988). We also used various back issues of the following magazines: *Fender Bridge, Fender Facts, Fender Frontline, Guitar Magazine* (UK), *Guitar Player, Guitar World, Guitarist, Making Music, Music Industry, Music Trades, One Two Testing.*